ISBN 0-8373-0565-9

C-565 CAREER EXAMINATION SERIES

This is your PASSBOOK® for...

Campus Security Guard I

Test Preparation Study Guide

Questions & Answers

NLC

NATIONAL LEARNING CORPORATION

Copyright © 2015 by

National Learning Corporation

212 Michael Drive, Syosset, New York 11791

All rights reserved, including the right of reproduction in whole or in part, in any form or by any means, electronic or mechanical, including photocopying, recording, or by any information storage and retrieval system, without permission in writing from the Publisher.

(516) 921-8888
(800) 645-6337
FAX: (516) 921-8743
www.passbooks.com
sales @ passbooks.com
info @ passbooks.com

PRINTED IN THE UNITED STATES OF AMERICA

PASSBOOK®
NOTICE

This book is SOLELY intended for, is sold ONLY to, and its use is RESTRICTED to *individual*, bona fide applicants or candidates who qualify by virtue of having seriously filed applications for appropriate license, certificate, professional and/or promotional advancement, higher school matriculation, scholarship, or other legitimate requirements of educational and/or governmental authorities.

This book is NOT intended for use, class instruction, tutoring, training, duplication, copying, reprinting, excerption, or adaptation, etc., by:

(1) Other publishers

(2) Proprietors and/or Instructors of "Coaching" and/or Preparatory Courses

(3) Personnel and/or Training Divisions of commercial, industrial, and governmental organizations

(4) Schools, colleges, or universities and/or their departments and staffs, including teachers and other personnel

(5) Testing Agencies or Bureaus

(6) Study groups which seek by the purchase of a single volume to copy and/or duplicate and/or adapt this material for use by the group as a whole without having purchased individual volumes for each of the members of the group

(7) Et al.

Such persons would be in violation of appropriate Federal and State statutes.

PROVISION OF LICENSING AGREEMENTS. — Recognized educational commercial, industrial, and governmental institutions and organizations, and others legitimately engaged in educational pursuits, including training, testing, and measurement activities, may address a request for a licensing agreement to the copyright owners, who will determine whether, and under what conditions, including fees and charges, the materials in this book may be used by them. In other words, a licensing facility exists for the legitimate use of the material in this book on other than an individual basis. However, it is asseverated and affirmed here that the material in this book *CANNOT* be used without the receipt of the express permission of such a licensing agreement from the Publishers.

NATIONAL LEARNING CORPORATION
212 Michael Drive
Syosset, New York 11791

Inquiries re licensing agreements should be addressed to:
The President
National Learning Corporation
212 Michael Drive
Syosset, New York 11791

PASSBOOK® SERIES

THE *PASSBOOK® SERIES* has been created to prepare applicants and candidates for the ultimate academic battlefield — the examination room.

At some time in our lives, each and every one of us may be required to take an examination — for validation, matriculation, admission, qualification, registration, certification, or licensure.

Based on the assumption that every applicant or candidate has met the basic formal educational standards, has taken the required number of courses, and read the necessary texts, the *PASSBOOK® SERIES* furnishes the one special preparation which may assure passing with confidence, instead of failing with insecurity. Examination questions — together with answers — are furnished as the basic vehicle for study so that the mysteries of the examination and its compounding difficulties may be eliminated or diminished by a sure method.

This book is meant to help you pass your examination provided that you qualify and are serious in your objective.

The entire field is reviewed through the huge store of content information which is succinctly presented through a provocative and challenging approach — the question-and-answer method.

A climate of success is established by furnishing the correct answers at the end of each test.

You soon learn to recognize types of questions, forms of questions, and patterns of questioning. You may even begin to anticipate expected outcomes.

You perceive that many questions are repeated or adapted so that you can gain acute insights, which may enable you to score many sure points.

You learn how to confront new questions, or types of questions, and to attack them confidently and work out the correct answers.

You note objectives and emphases, and recognize pitfalls and dangers, so that you may make positive educational adjustments.

Moreover, you are kept fully informed in relation to new concepts, methods, practices, and directions in the field.

You discover that you are actually taking the examination all the time: you are preparing for the examination by "taking" an examination, not by reading extraneous and/or supererogatory textbooks.

In short, this PASSBOOK®, used directedly, should be an important factor in helping you to pass your test.

CAMPUS SECURITY GUARD I

DUTIES
Patrols buildings and grounds to prevent trespassing and damage to property and to maintain general public order. Patrols parking lots and issues citations for illegal parking. Greets the public and directs them to buildings and exhibits during open house, commencement exercises, registration, orientation, and other campus activities which are open to the public. Controls traffic, writes detailed description of accidents, and assists those involved. Performs related work as required.

SCOPE OF THE EXAMINATION
The <u>multiple choice</u> test will cover knowledge's, skills, and/or abilities in such areas as;
1. Understanding and interpreting legal passages;
2. Using good judgment in situations involving public safety; and
3. Preparing written material.

HOW TO TAKE A TEST

I. YOU MUST PASS AN EXAMINATION

A. *WHAT EVERY CANDIDATE SHOULD KNOW*

Examination applicants often ask us for help in preparing for the written test. What can I study in advance? What kinds of questions will be asked? How will the test be given? How will the papers be graded?

As an applicant for a civil service examination, you may be wondering about some of these things. Our purpose here is to suggest effective methods of advance study and to describe civil service examinations.

Your chances for success on this examination can be increased if you know how to prepare. Those "pre-examination jitters" can be reduced if you know what to expect. You can even experience an adventure in good citizenship if you know why civil service exams are given.

B. *WHY ARE CIVIL SERVICE EXAMINATIONS GIVEN?*

Civil service examinations are important to you in two ways. As a citizen, you want public jobs filled by employees who know how to do their work. As a job seeker, you want a fair chance to compete for that job on an equal footing with other candidates. The best-known means of accomplishing this two-fold goal is the competitive examination.

Exams are widely publicized throughout the nation. They may be administered for jobs in federal, state, city, municipal, town or village governments or agencies.

Any citizen may apply, with some limitations, such as the age or residence of applicants. Your experience and education may be reviewed to see whether you meet the requirements for the particular examination. When these requirements exist, they are reasonable and applied consistently to all applicants. Thus, a competitive examination may cause you some uneasiness now, but it is your privilege and safeguard.

C. *HOW ARE CIVIL SERVICE EXAMS DEVELOPED?*

Examinations are carefully written by trained technicians who are specialists in the field known as "psychological measurement," in consultation with recognized authorities in the field of work that the test will cover. These experts recommend the subject matter areas or skills to be tested; only those knowledges or skills important to your success on the job are included. The most reliable books and source materials available are used as references. Together, the experts and technicians judge the difficulty level of the questions.

Test technicians know how to phrase questions so that the problem is clearly stated. Their ethics do not permit "trick" or "catch" questions. Questions may have been tried out on sample groups, or subjected to statistical analysis, to determine their usefulness.

Written tests are often used in combination with performance tests, ratings of training and experience, and oral interviews. All of these measures combine to form the best-known means of finding the right person for the right job.

II. HOW TO PASS THE WRITTEN TEST

A. NATURE OF THE EXAMINATION

To prepare intelligently for civil service examinations, you should know how they differ from school examinations you have taken. In school you were assigned certain definite pages to read or subjects to cover. The examination questions were quite detailed and usually emphasized memory. Civil service exams, on the other hand, try to discover your present ability to perform the duties of a position, plus your potentiality to learn these duties. In other words, a civil service exam attempts to predict how successful you will be. Questions cover such a broad area that they cannot be as minute and detailed as school exam questions.

In the public service similar kinds of work, or positions, are grouped together in one "class." This process is known as *position-classification*. All the positions in a class are paid according to the salary range for that class. One class title covers all of these positions, and they are all tested by the same examination.

B. FOUR BASIC STEPS

1) Study the announcement

How, then, can you know what subjects to study? Our best answer is: "Learn as much as possible about the class of positions for which you've applied." The exam will test the knowledge, skills and abilities needed to do the work.

Your most valuable source of information about the position you want is the official exam announcement. This announcement lists the training and experience qualifications. Check these standards and apply only if you come reasonably close to meeting them.

The brief description of the position in the examination announcement offers some clues to the subjects which will be tested. Think about the job itself. Review the duties in your mind. Can you perform them, or are there some in which you are rusty? Fill in the blank spots in your preparation.

Many jurisdictions preview the written test in the exam announcement by including a section called "Knowledge and Abilities Required," "Scope of the Examination," or some similar heading. Here you will find out specifically what fields will be tested.

2) Review your own background

Once you learn in general what the position is all about, and what you need to know to do the work, ask yourself which subjects you already know fairly well and which need improvement. You may wonder whether to concentrate on improving your strong areas or on building some background in your fields of weakness. When the announcement has specified "some knowledge" or "considerable knowledge," or has used adjectives like "beginning principles of..." or "advanced ... methods," you can get a clue as to the number and difficulty of questions to be asked in any given field. More questions, and hence broader coverage, would be included for those subjects which are more important in the work. Now weigh your strengths and weaknesses against the job requirements and prepare accordingly.

3) Determine the level of the position

Another way to tell how intensively you should prepare is to understand the level of the job for which you are applying. Is it the entering level? In other words, is this the position in which beginners in a field of work are hired? Or is it an intermediate or advanced level? Sometimes this is indicated by such words as "Junior" or "Senior" in the class title. Other jurisdictions use Roman numerals to designate the level – Clerk I, Clerk II, for example. The word "Supervisor" sometimes appears in the title. If the level is not indicated by the title, check the description of duties. Will you be working under very close supervision, or will you have responsibility for independent decisions in this work?

4) Choose appropriate study materials

Now that you know the subjects to be examined and the relative amount of each subject to be covered, you can choose suitable study materials. For beginning level jobs, or even advanced ones, if you have a pronounced weakness in some aspect of your training, read a modern, standard textbook in that field. Be sure it is up to date and has general coverage. Such books are normally available at your library, and the librarian will be glad to help you locate one. For entry-level positions, questions of appropriate difficulty are chosen – neither highly advanced questions, nor those too simple. Such questions require careful thought but not advanced training.

If the position for which you are applying is technical or advanced, you will read more advanced, specialized material. If you are already familiar with the basic principles of your field, elementary textbooks would waste your time. Concentrate on advanced textbooks and technical periodicals. Think through the concepts and review difficult problems in your field.

These are all general sources. You can get more ideas on your own initiative, following these leads. For example, training manuals and publications of the government agency which employs workers in your field can be useful, particularly for technical and professional positions. A letter or visit to the government department involved may result in more specific study suggestions, and certainly will provide you with a more definite idea of the exact nature of the position you are seeking.

III. KINDS OF TESTS

Tests are used for purposes other than measuring knowledge and ability to perform specified duties. For some positions, it is equally important to test ability to make adjustments to new situations or to profit from training. In others, basic mental abilities not dependent on information are essential. Questions which test these things may not appear as pertinent to the duties of the position as those which test for knowledge and information. Yet they are often highly important parts of a fair examination. For very general questions, it is almost impossible to help you direct your study efforts. What we can do is to point out some of the more common of these general abilities needed in public service positions and describe some typical questions.

1) General information

Broad, general information has been found useful for predicting job success in some kinds of work. This is tested in a variety of ways, from vocabulary lists to questions about current events. Basic background in some field of work, such as sociology or economics, may be sampled in a group of questions. Often these are principles which have become familiar to most persons through exposure rather than through formal training. It is difficult to advise you how to study for these questions; being alert to the world around you is our best suggestion.

2) Verbal ability

An example of an ability needed in many positions is verbal or language ability. Verbal ability is, in brief, the ability to use and understand words. Vocabulary and grammar tests are typical measures of this ability. Reading comprehension or paragraph interpretation questions are common in many kinds of civil service tests. You are given a paragraph of written material and asked to find its central meaning.

3) Numerical ability

Number skills can be tested by the familiar arithmetic problem, by checking paired lists of numbers to see which are alike and which are different, or by interpreting charts and graphs. In the latter test, a graph may be printed in the test booklet which you are asked to use as the basis for answering questions.

4) Observation

A popular test for law-enforcement positions is the observation test. A picture is shown to you for several minutes, then taken away. Questions about the picture test your ability to observe both details and larger elements.

5) Following directions

In many positions in the public service, the employee must be able to carry out written instructions dependably and accurately. You may be given a chart with several columns, each column listing a variety of information. The questions require you to carry out directions involving the information given in the chart.

6) Skills and aptitudes

Performance tests effectively measure some manual skills and aptitudes. When the skill is one in which you are trained, such as typing or shorthand, you can practice. These tests are often very much like those given in business school or high school courses. For many of the other skills and aptitudes, however, no short-time preparation can be made. Skills and abilities natural to you or that you have developed throughout your lifetime are being tested.

Many of the general questions just described provide all the data needed to answer the questions and ask you to use your reasoning ability to find the answers. Your best preparation for these tests, as well as for tests of facts and ideas, is to be at your physical and mental best. You, no doubt, have your own methods of getting into an exam-taking mood and keeping "in shape." The next section lists some ideas on this subject.

IV. KINDS OF QUESTIONS

Only rarely is the "essay" question, which you answer in narrative form, used in civil service tests. Civil service tests are usually of the short-answer type. Full instructions for answering these questions will be given to you at the examination. But in case this is your first experience with short-answer questions and separate answer sheets, here is what you need to know:

1) Multiple-choice Questions

Most popular of the short-answer questions is the "multiple choice" or "best answer" question. It can be used, for example, to test for factual knowledge, ability to solve problems or judgment in meeting situations found at work.

A multiple-choice question is normally one of three types—
- It can begin with an incomplete statement followed by several possible endings. You are to find the one ending which *best* completes the statement, although some of the others may not be entirely wrong.
- It can also be a complete statement in the form of a question which is answered by choosing one of the statements listed.
- It can be in the form of a problem – again you select the best answer.

Here is an example of a multiple-choice question with a discussion which should give you some clues as to the method for choosing the right answer:

When an employee has a complaint about his assignment, the action which will *best* help him overcome his difficulty is to
    A. discuss his difficulty with his coworkers
    B. take the problem to the head of the organization
    C. take the problem to the person who gave him the assignment
    D. say nothing to anyone about his complaint

In answering this question, you should study each of the choices to find which is best. Consider choice "A" – Certainly an employee may discuss his complaint with fellow employees, but no change or improvement can result, and the complaint remains unresolved. Choice "B" is a poor choice since the head of the organization probably does not know what assignment you have been given, and taking your problem to him is known as "going over the head" of the supervisor. The supervisor, or person who made the assignment, is the person who can clarify it or correct any injustice. Choice "C" is, therefore, correct. To say nothing, as in choice "D," is unwise. Supervisors have and interest in knowing the problems employees are facing, and the employee is seeking a solution to his problem.

2) True/False Questions

The "true/false" or "right/wrong" form of question is sometimes used. Here a complete statement is given. Your job is to decide whether the statement is right or wrong.

SAMPLE: A person-to-person long-distance telephone call costs less than a station-to-station call to the same city.

This statement is wrong, or false, since person-to-person calls are more expensive.

This is not a complete list of all possible question forms, although most of the others are variations of these common types. You will always get complete directions for answering questions. Be sure you understand *how* to mark your answers – ask questions until you do.

V. RECORDING YOUR ANSWERS

For an examination with very few applicants, you may be told to record your answers in the test booklet itself. Separate answer sheets are much more common. If this separate answer sheet is to be scored by machine – and this is often the case – it is highly important that you mark your answers correctly in order to get credit.

An electric scoring machine is often used in civil service offices because of the speed with which papers can be scored. Machine-scored answer sheets must be marked with a pencil, which will be given to you. This pencil has a high graphite content which responds to the electric scoring machine. As a matter of fact, stray dots may register as answers, so do not let your pencil rest on the answer sheet while you are pondering the correct answer. Also, if your pencil lead breaks or is otherwise defective, ask for another.

Since the answer sheet will be dropped in a slot in the scoring machine, be careful not to bend the corners or get the paper crumpled.

The answer sheet normally has five vertical columns of numbers, with 30 numbers to a column. These numbers correspond to the question numbers in your test booklet. After each number, going across the page are four or five pairs of dotted lines. These short dotted lines have small letters or numbers above them. The first two pairs may also have a "T" or "F" above the letters. This indicates that the first two pairs only are to be used if the questions are of the true-false type. If the questions are multiple choice, disregard the "T" and "F" and pay attention only to the small letters or numbers.

Answer your questions in the manner of the sample that follows:

32. The largest city in the United States is
    A. Washington, D.C.
    B. New York City
    C. Chicago
    D. Detroit
    E. San Francisco

1) Choose the answer you think is best. (New York City is the largest, so "B" is correct.)
2) Find the row of dotted lines numbered the same as the question you are answering. (Find row number 32)
3) Find the pair of dotted lines corresponding to the answer. (Find the pair of lines under the mark "B.")
4) Make a solid black mark between the dotted lines.

VI. BEFORE THE TEST

Common sense will help you find procedures to follow to get ready for an examination. Too many of us, however, overlook these sensible measures. Indeed, nervousness and fatigue have been found to be the most serious reasons why applicants fail to do their best on civil service tests. Here is a list of reminders:

- Begin your preparation early – Don't wait until the last minute to go scurrying around for books and materials or to find out what the position is all about.
- Prepare continuously – An hour a night for a week is better than an all-night cram session. This has been definitely established. What is more, a night a

week for a month will return better dividends than crowding your study into a shorter period of time.
- Locate the place of the exam – You have been sent a notice telling you when and where to report for the examination. If the location is in a different town or otherwise unfamiliar to you, it would be well to inquire the best route and learn something about the building.
- Relax the night before the test – Allow your mind to rest. Do not study at all that night. Plan some mild recreation or diversion; then go to bed early and get a good night's sleep.
- Get up early enough to make a leisurely trip to the place for the test – This way unforeseen events, traffic snarls, unfamiliar buildings, etc. will not upset you.
- Dress comfortably – A written test is not a fashion show. You will be known by number and not by name, so wear something comfortable.
- Leave excess paraphernalia at home – Shopping bags and odd bundles will get in your way. You need bring only the items mentioned in the official notice you received; usually everything you need is provided. Do not bring reference books to the exam. They will only confuse those last minutes and be taken away from you when in the test room.
- Arrive somewhat ahead of time – If because of transportation schedules you must get there very early, bring a newspaper or magazine to take your mind off yourself while waiting.
- Locate the examination room – When you have found the proper room, you will be directed to the seat or part of the room where you will sit. Sometimes you are given a sheet of instructions to read while you are waiting. Do not fill out any forms until you are told to do so; just read them and be prepared.
- Relax and prepare to listen to the instructions
- If you have any physical problem that may keep you from doing your best, be sure to tell the test administrator. If you are sick or in poor health, you really cannot do your best on the exam. You can come back and take the test some other time.

VII. AT THE TEST

The day of the test is here and you have the test booklet in your hand. The temptation to get going is very strong. Caution! There is more to success than knowing the right answers. You must know how to identify your papers and understand variations in the type of short-answer question used in this particular examination. Follow these suggestions for maximum results from your efforts:

1) Cooperate with the monitor
The test administrator has a duty to create a situation in which you can be as much at ease as possible. He will give instructions, tell you when to begin, check to see that you are marking your answer sheet correctly, and so on. He is not there to guard you, although he will see that your competitors do not take unfair advantage. He wants to help you do your best.

2) Listen to all instructions
Don't jump the gun! Wait until you understand all directions. In most civil service tests you get more time than you need to answer the questions. So don't be in a hurry.

Read each word of instructions until you clearly understand the meaning. Study the examples, listen to all announcements and follow directions. Ask questions if you do not understand what to do.

3) Identify your papers

Civil service exams are usually identified by number only. You will be assigned a number; you must not put your name on your test papers. Be sure to copy your number correctly. Since more than one exam may be given, copy your exact examination title.

4) Plan your time

Unless you are told that a test is a "speed" or "rate of work" test, speed itself is usually not important. Time enough to answer all the questions will be provided, but this does not mean that you have all day. An overall time limit has been set. Divide the total time (in minutes) by the number of questions to determine the approximate time you have for each question.

5) Do not linger over difficult questions

If you come across a difficult question, mark it with a paper clip (useful to have along) and come back to it when you have been through the booklet. One caution if you do this – be sure to skip a number on your answer sheet as well. Check often to be sure that you have not lost your place and that you are marking in the row numbered the same as the question you are answering.

6) Read the questions

Be sure you know what the question asks! Many capable people are unsuccessful because they failed to *read* the questions correctly.

7) Answer all questions

Unless you have been instructed that a penalty will be deducted for incorrect answers, it is better to guess than to omit a question.

8) Speed tests

It is often better NOT to guess on speed tests. It has been found that on timed tests people are tempted to spend the last few seconds before time is called in marking answers at random – without even reading them – in the hope of picking up a few extra points. To discourage this practice, the instructions may warn you that your score will be "corrected" for guessing. That is, a penalty will be applied. The incorrect answers will be deducted from the correct ones, or some other penalty formula will be used.

9) Review your answers

If you finish before time is called, go back to the questions you guessed or omitted to give them further thought. Review other answers if you have time.

10) Return your test materials

If you are ready to leave before others have finished or time is called, take ALL your materials to the monitor and leave quietly. Never take any test material with you. The monitor can discover whose papers are not complete, and taking a test booklet may be grounds for disqualification.

VIII. EXAMINATION TECHNIQUES

1) Read the general instructions carefully. These are usually printed on the first page of the exam booklet. As a rule, these instructions refer to the timing of the examination; the fact that you should not start work until the signal and must stop work at a signal, etc. If there are any *special* instructions, such as a choice of questions to be answered, make sure that you note this instruction carefully.

2) When you are ready to start work on the examination, that is as soon as the signal has been given, read the instructions to each question booklet, underline any key words or phrases, such as *least, best, outline, describe* and the like. In this way you will tend to answer as requested rather than discover on reviewing your paper that you *listed without describing*, that you selected the *worst* choice rather than the *best* choice, etc.

3) If the examination is of the objective or multiple-choice type – that is, each question will also give a series of possible answers: A, B, C or D, and you are called upon to select the best answer and write the letter next to that answer on your answer paper – it is advisable to start answering each question in turn. There may be anywhere from 50 to 100 such questions in the three or four hours allotted and you can see how much time would be taken if you read through all the questions before beginning to answer any. Furthermore, if you come across a question or group of questions which you know would be difficult to answer, it would undoubtedly affect your handling of all the other questions.

4) If the examination is of the essay type and contains but a few questions, it is a moot point as to whether you should read all the questions before starting to answer any one. Of course, if you are given a choice – say five out of seven and the like – then it is essential to read all the questions so you can eliminate the two that are most difficult. If, however, you are asked to answer all the questions, there may be danger in trying to answer the easiest one first because you may find that you will spend too much time on it. The best technique is to answer the first question, then proceed to the second, etc.

5) Time your answers. Before the exam begins, write down the time it started, then add the time allowed for the examination and write down the time it must be completed, then divide the time available somewhat as follows:
   - If 3-1/2 hours are allowed, that would be 210 minutes. If you have 80 objective-type questions, that would be an average of 2-1/2 minutes per question. Allow yourself no more than 2 minutes per question, or a total of 160 minutes, which will permit about 50 minutes to review.
   - If for the time allotment of 210 minutes there are 7 essay questions to answer, that would average about 30 minutes a question. Give yourself only 25 minutes per question so that you have about 35 minutes to review.

6) The most important instruction is to *read each question* and make sure you know what is wanted. The second most important instruction is to *time yourself properly* so that you answer every question. The third most

important instruction is to *answer every question*. Guess if you have to but include something for each question. Remember that you will receive no credit for a blank and will probably receive some credit if you write something in answer to an essay question. If you guess a letter – say "B" for a multiple-choice question – you may have guessed right. If you leave a blank as an answer to a multiple-choice question, the examiners may respect your feelings but it will not add a point to your score. Some exams may penalize you for wrong answers, so in such cases *only*, you may not want to guess unless you have some basis for your answer.

7) Suggestions
   a. Objective-type questions
      1. Examine the question booklet for proper sequence of pages and questions
      2. Read all instructions carefully
      3. Skip any question which seems too difficult; return to it after all other questions have been answered
      4. Apportion your time properly; do not spend too much time on any single question or group of questions
      5. Note and underline key words – *all, most, fewest, least, best, worst, same, opposite,* etc.
      6. Pay particular attention to negatives
      7. Note unusual option, e.g., unduly long, short, complex, different or similar in content to the body of the question
      8. Observe the use of "hedging" words – *probably, may, most likely,* etc.
      9. Make sure that your answer is put next to the same number as the question
      10. Do not second-guess unless you have good reason to believe the second answer is definitely more correct
      11. Cross out original answer if you decide another answer is more accurate; do not erase until you are ready to hand your paper in
      12. Answer all questions; guess unless instructed otherwise
      13. Leave time for review

   b. Essay questions
      1. Read each question carefully
      2. Determine exactly what is wanted. Underline key words or phrases.
      3. Decide on outline or paragraph answer
      4. Include many different points and elements unless asked to develop any one or two points or elements
      5. Show impartiality by giving pros and cons unless directed to select one side only
      6. Make and write down any assumptions you find necessary to answer the questions
      7. Watch your English, grammar, punctuation and choice of words
      8. Time your answers; don't crowd material

8) Answering the essay question

Most essay questions can be answered by framing the specific response around several key words or ideas. Here are a few such key words or ideas:

M's: manpower, materials, methods, money, management
P's: purpose, program, policy, plan, procedure, practice, problems, pitfalls, personnel, public relations

   a. Six basic steps in handling problems:
      1. Preliminary plan and background development
      2. Collect information, data and facts
      3. Analyze and interpret information, data and facts
      4. Analyze and develop solutions as well as make recommendations
      5. Prepare report and sell recommendations
      6. Install recommendations and follow up effectiveness

   b. Pitfalls to avoid
      1. *Taking things for granted* – A statement of the situation does not necessarily imply that each of the elements is necessarily true; for example, a complaint may be invalid and biased so that all that can be taken for granted is that a complaint has been registered
      2. *Considering only one side of a situation* – Wherever possible, indicate several alternatives and then point out the reasons you selected the best one
      3. *Failing to indicate follow up* – Whenever your answer indicates action on your part, make certain that you will take proper follow-up action to see how successful your recommendations, procedures or actions turn out to be
      4. *Taking too long in answering any single question* – Remember to time your answers properly

IX. AFTER THE TEST

Scoring procedures differ in detail among civil service jurisdictions although the general principles are the same. Whether the papers are hand-scored or graded by machine we have described, they are nearly always graded by number. That is, the person who marks the paper knows only the number – never the name – of the applicant. Not until all the papers have been graded will they be matched with names. If other tests, such as training and experience or oral interview ratings have been given, scores will be combined. Different parts of the examination usually have different weights. For example, the written test might count 60 percent of the final grade, and a rating of training and experience 40 percent. In many jurisdictions, veterans will have a certain number of points added to their grades.

After the final grade has been determined, the names are placed in grade order and an eligible list is established. There are various methods for resolving ties between those who get the same final grade – probably the most common is to place first the name of the person whose application was received first. Job offers are made from the eligible list in the order the names appear on it. You will be notified of your grade and your rank as soon as all these computations have been made. This will be done as rapidly as possible.

People who are found to meet the requirements in the announcement are called "eligibles." Their names are put on a list of eligible candidates. An eligible's chances of getting a job depend on how high he stands on this list and how fast agencies are filling jobs from the list.

When a job is to be filled from a list of eligibles, the agency asks for the names of people on the list of eligibles for that job. When the civil service commission receives this request, it sends to the agency the names of the three people highest on this list. Or, if the job to be filled has specialized requirements, the office sends the agency the names of the top three persons who meet these requirements from the general list.

The appointing officer makes a choice from among the three people whose names were sent to him. If the selected person accepts the appointment, the names of the others are put back on the list to be considered for future openings.

That is the rule in hiring from all kinds of eligible lists, whether they are for typist, carpenter, chemist, or something else. For every vacancy, the appointing officer has his choice of any one of the top three eligibles on the list. This explains why the person whose name is on top of the list sometimes does not get an appointment when some of the persons lower on the list do. If the appointing officer chooses the second or third eligible, the No. 1 eligible does not get a job at once, but stays on the list until he is appointed or the list is terminated.

X. HOW TO PASS THE INTERVIEW TEST

The examination for which you applied requires an oral interview test. You have already taken the written test and you are now being called for the interview test – the final part of the formal examination.

You may think that it is not possible to prepare for an interview test and that there are no procedures to follow during an interview. Our purpose is to point out some things you can do in advance that will help you and some good rules to follow and pitfalls to avoid while you are being interviewed.

What is an interview supposed to test?

The written examination is designed to test the technical knowledge and competence of the candidate; the oral is designed to evaluate intangible qualities, not readily measured otherwise, and to establish a list showing the relative fitness of each candidate – as measured against his competitors – for the position sought. Scoring is not on the basis of "right" and "wrong," but on a sliding scale of values ranging from "not passable" to "outstanding." As a matter of fact, it is possible to achieve a relatively low score without a single "incorrect" answer because of evident weakness in the qualities being measured.

Occasionally, an examination may consist entirely of an oral test – either an individual or a group oral. In such cases, information is sought concerning the technical knowledges and abilities of the candidate, since there has been no written examination for this purpose. More commonly, however, an oral test is used to supplement a written examination.

Who conducts interviews?

The composition of oral boards varies among different jurisdictions. In nearly all, a representative of the personnel department serves as chairman. One of the members of the board may be a representative of the department in which the candidate would work. In some cases, "outside experts" are used, and, frequently, a businessman or some other representative of the general public is asked to serve. Labor and management or other special groups may be represented. The aim is to secure the services of experts in the appropriate field.

However the board is composed, it is a good idea (and not at all improper or unethical) to ascertain in advance of the interview who the members are and what groups they represent. When you are introduced to them, you will have some idea of their backgrounds and interests, and at least you will not stutter and stammer over their names.

What should be done before the interview?

While knowledge about the board members is useful and takes some of the surprise element out of the interview, there is other preparation which is more substantive. It *is* possible to prepare for an oral interview – in several ways:

1) Keep a copy of your application and review it carefully before the interview

This may be the only document before the oral board, and the starting point of the interview. Know what education and experience you have listed there, and the sequence and dates of all of it. Sometimes the board will ask you to review the highlights of your experience for them; you should not have to hem and haw doing it.

2) Study the class specification and the examination announcement

Usually, the oral board has one or both of these to guide them. The qualities, characteristics or knowledges required by the position sought are stated in these documents. They offer valuable clues as to the nature of the oral interview. For example, if the job involves supervisory responsibilities, the announcement will usually indicate that knowledge of modern supervisory methods and the qualifications of the candidate as a supervisor will be tested. If so, you can expect such questions, frequently in the form of a hypothetical situation which you are expected to solve. NEVER go into an oral without knowledge of the duties and responsibilities of the job you seek.

3) Think through each qualification required

Try to visualize the kind of questions you would ask if you were a board member. How well could you answer them? Try especially to appraise your own knowledge and background in each area, *measured against the job sought*, and identify any areas in which you are weak. Be critical and realistic – do not flatter yourself.

4) Do some general reading in areas in which you feel you may be weak

For example, if the job involves supervision and your past experience has NOT, some general reading in supervisory methods and practices, particularly in the field of human relations, might be useful. Do NOT study agency procedures or detailed manuals. The oral board will be testing your understanding and capacity, not your memory.

5) Get a good night's sleep and watch your general health and mental attitude

You will want a clear head at the interview. Take care of a cold or any other minor ailment, and of course, no hangovers.

What should be done on the day of the interview?

Now comes the day of the interview itself. Give yourself plenty of time to get there. Plan to arrive somewhat ahead of the scheduled time, particularly if your appointment is in the fore part of the day. If a previous candidate fails to appear, the board might be ready for you a bit early. By early afternoon an oral board is almost invariably behind schedule if there are many candidates, and you may have to wait.

Take along a book or magazine to read, or your application to review, but leave any extraneous material in the waiting room when you go in for your interview. In any event, relax and compose yourself.

The matter of dress is important. The board is forming impressions about you – from your experience, your manners, your attitude, and your appearance. Give your personal appearance careful attention. Dress your best, but not your flashiest. Choose conservative, appropriate clothing, and be sure it is immaculate. This is a business interview, and your appearance should indicate that you regard it as such. Besides, being well groomed and properly dressed will help boost your confidence.

Sooner or later, someone will call your name and escort you into the interview room. *This is it.* From here on you are on your own. It is too late for any more preparation. But remember, you asked for this opportunity to prove your fitness, and you are here because your request was granted.

What happens when you go in?

The usual sequence of events will be as follows: The clerk (who is often the board stenographer) will introduce you to the chairman of the oral board, who will introduce you to the other members of the board. Acknowledge the introductions before you sit down. Do not be surprised if you find a microphone facing you or a stenotypist sitting by. Oral interviews are usually recorded in the event of an appeal or other review.

Usually the chairman of the board will open the interview by reviewing the highlights of your education and work experience from your application – primarily for the benefit of the other members of the board, as well as to get the material into the record. Do not interrupt or comment unless there is an error or significant misinterpretation; if that is the case, do not hesitate. But do not quibble about insignificant matters. Also, he will usually ask you some question about your education, experience or your present job – partly to get you to start talking and to establish the interviewing "rapport." He may start the actual questioning, or turn it over to one of the other members. Frequently, each member undertakes the questioning on a particular area, one in which he is perhaps most competent, so you can expect each member to participate in the examination. Because time is limited, you may also expect some rather abrupt switches in the direction the questioning takes, so do not be upset by it. Normally, a board member will not pursue a single line of questioning unless he discovers a particular strength or weakness.

After each member has participated, the chairman will usually ask whether any member has any further questions, then will ask you if you have anything you wish to add. Unless you are expecting this question, it may floor you. Worse, it may start you off on an extended, extemporaneous speech. The board is not usually seeking more information. The question is principally to offer you a last opportunity to present further qualifications or to indicate that you have nothing to add. So, if you feel that a significant qualification or characteristic has been overlooked, it is proper to point it out in a sentence or so. Do not compliment the board on the thoroughness of their examination – they have been sketchy, and you know it. If you wish, merely say, "No thank you, I have nothing further to add." This is a point where you can "talk yourself out" of a good impression or fail to present an important bit of information. Remember, *you close the interview yourself.*

The chairman will then say, "That is all, Mr. _____, thank you." Do not be startled; the interview is over, and quicker than you think. Thank him, gather your belongings and take your leave. Save your sigh of relief for the other side of the door.

How to put your best foot forward

Throughout this entire process, you may feel that the board individually and collectively is trying to pierce your defenses, seek out your hidden weaknesses and embarrass and confuse you. Actually, this is not true. They are obliged to make an appraisal of your qualifications for the job you are seeking, and they want to see you in your best light. Remember, they must interview all candidates and a non-cooperative candidate may become a failure in spite of their best efforts to bring out his qualifications. Here are 15 suggestions that will help you:

1) Be natural – Keep your attitude confident, not cocky

If you are not confident that you can do the job, do not expect the board to be. Do not apologize for your weaknesses, try to bring out your strong points. The board is interested in a positive, not negative, presentation. Cockiness will antagonize any board member and make him wonder if you are covering up a weakness by a false show of strength.

2) Get comfortable, but don't lounge or sprawl

Sit erectly but not stiffly. A careless posture may lead the board to conclude that you are careless in other things, or at least that you are not impressed by the importance of the occasion. Either conclusion is natural, even if incorrect. Do not fuss with your clothing, a pencil or an ashtray. Your hands may occasionally be useful to emphasize a point; do not let them become a point of distraction.

3) Do not wisecrack or make small talk

This is a serious situation, and your attitude should show that you consider it as such. Further, the time of the board is limited – they do not want to waste it, and neither should you.

4) Do not exaggerate your experience or abilities

In the first place, from information in the application or other interviews and sources, the board may know more about you than you think. Secondly, you probably will not get away with it. An experienced board is rather adept at spotting such a situation, so do not take the chance.

5) If you know a board member, do not make a point of it, yet do not hide it

Certainly you are not fooling him, and probably not the other members of the board. Do not try to take advantage of your acquaintanceship – it will probably do you little good.

6) Do not dominate the interview

Let the board do that. They will give you the clues – do not assume that you have to do all the talking. Realize that the board has a number of questions to ask you, and do not try to take up all the interview time by showing off your extensive knowledge of the answer to the first one.

7) Be attentive

You only have 20 minutes or so, and you should keep your attention at its sharpest throughout. When a member is addressing a problem or question to you, give him your undivided attention. Address your reply principally to him, but do not exclude the other board members.

8) Do not interrupt

A board member may be stating a problem for you to analyze. He will ask you a question when the time comes. Let him state the problem, and wait for the question.

9) Make sure you understand the question

Do not try to answer until you are sure what the question is. If it is not clear, restate it in your own words or ask the board member to clarify it for you. However, do not haggle about minor elements.

10) Reply promptly but not hastily

A common entry on oral board rating sheets is "candidate responded readily," or "candidate hesitated in replies." Respond as promptly and quickly as you can, but do not jump to a hasty, ill-considered answer.

11) Do not be peremptory in your answers

A brief answer is proper – but do not fire your answer back. That is a losing game from your point of view. The board member can probably ask questions much faster than you can answer them.

12) Do not try to create the answer you think the board member wants

He is interested in what kind of mind you have and how it works – not in playing games. Furthermore, he can usually spot this practice and will actually grade you down on it.

13) Do not switch sides in your reply merely to agree with a board member

Frequently, a member will take a contrary position merely to draw you out and to see if you are willing and able to defend your point of view. Do not start a debate, yet do not surrender a good position. If a position is worth taking, it is worth defending.

14) Do not be afraid to admit an error in judgment if you are shown to be wrong

The board knows that you are forced to reply without any opportunity for careful consideration. Your answer may be demonstrably wrong. If so, admit it and get on with the interview.

15) Do not dwell at length on your present job

The opening question may relate to your present assignment. Answer the question but do not go into an extended discussion. You are being examined for a *new* job, not your present one. As a matter of fact, try to phrase ALL your answers in terms of the job for which you are being examined.

Basis of Rating

Probably you will forget most of these "do's" and "don'ts" when you walk into the oral interview room. Even remembering them all will not ensure you a passing grade. Perhaps you did not have the qualifications in the first place. But remembering them will help you to put your best foot forward, without treading on the toes of the board members.

Rumor and popular opinion to the contrary notwithstanding, an oral board wants you to make the best appearance possible. They know you are under pressure – but they also want to see how you respond to it as a guide to what your reaction would be under the pressures of the job you seek. They will be influenced by the degree of poise you display, the personal traits you show and the manner in which you respond.

EXAMINATION SECTION

EXAMINATION SECTION
TEST 1

DIRECTIONS: Questions 1 through 5 are to be answered on the basis of the information, instructions, and sample question given below. Each question contains a GENERAL RULE, EXCEPTIONS, a PROBLEM, and the ACTION actually taken.

The GENERAL RULE explains what the special officer (security officer) should or should not do.

The EXCEPTIONS describe circumstances under which a special officer (security officer) should take action contrary to the GENERAL RULE.

However, an unusual emergency may justify taking an action that is not covered either by the GENERAL RULE or by the stated EXCEPTIONS.

The PROBLEM describes a situation requiring some action by the special officer (security officer).

ACTION describes what a special officer (security officer) actually did in that particular case.

Read carefully the GENERAL RULE and EXCEPTIONS, the PROBLEM, and the ACTION, and the mark A, B, C, or D in the space at the right in accordance with the following instructions:

  I. If an action is clearly justified under the general rule, mark your answer A.
  II. If an action is not justified under the general rule, but is justified under a stated exception, mark your answer B.
  III. If an action is not justified either by the general rule or by a stated exception, but does seem strongly justified by an unusual emergency situation, mark your answer C.
  IV. If an action does not seem justified for any of these reasons, mark your answer D.

SAMPLE QUESTION:

GENERAL RULE: A special officer (security officer) is not empowered to stop a person and search him for hidden weapons.
EXCEPTION: He may stop a person and search him if he has good reason to believe that he may be carrying a hidden weapon. Good reasons to believe he may be carrying a hidden weapon include (a) notification through official channels that a person may be armed, (b) a statement directly to the special officer (security officer) by the person himself that he is armed, and (c) the special officer's (security officer's) own direct observation.

PROBLEM: A special officer (security officer) on duty at a hospital clinic is notified by a woman patient at the clinic that a man sitting near her is making muttered threats that he has a gun and is going to shoot his doctor if the doctor gives him any trouble. Although the woman is upset, she seems to be telling the truth, and two other waiting patients con-

firm this. However, the special officer (security officer) approaches the man and sees no sign of a hidden weapon. The man tells the officer that he has no weapon.
ACTION: The special officer (security officer) takes the man aside into an empty office and proceeds to frisk him for a concealed weapon.

ANSWER: The answer cannot be A, because the general rule is that a special officer (security officer) is not empowered to search a person for hidden weapons. The answer cannot be B, because the notification did not come through official channels, the man did not tell the special officer (security officer) that he had a weapon, and the special officer (security officer) did not observe any weapon. However, since three people have confirmed that the man has said he has a weapon and is threatening to use it, this is pretty clearly an emergency situation that calls for action. Therefore, the answer is C.

1. GENERAL RULE: A special officer (security officer) on duty at a certain entrance is not to leave his post unguarded at any time.
   EXCEPTION: He may leave the post for a brief period if he first summons a replacement. He may also leave if it is necessary for him to take prompt emergency action to prevent injury to persons or property.
   PROBLEM: The special officer (security officer) sees a man running down a hall with a piece of iron pipe in his hand, chasing another man who is shouting for help. By going in immediate pursuit, there is a good chance that the special officer (security officer) can stop the man with the pipe.
   ACTION: The special officer (security officer) leaves his post unguarded and pursues the man.

   The CORRECT answer is:

   A. I   B. II   C. III   D. IV

2. GENERAL RULE: Special officers (security officers) assigned to a college campus are instructed not to arrest students for minor violations such as disorderly conduct; instead, the violation should be stopped and the incident should be reported to the college authorities, who will take disciplinary action.
   EXCEPTION: A special officer (security officer) may arrest a student or take other appropriate action if failure to do so is likely to result in personal injury or property damage, or disruption of school activities, or if the incident involves serious criminal behavior.
   PROBLEM: A special officer (security officer) is on duty in a college building where evening classes are being held. He is told that two students are causing a disturbance in a classroom. He arrives and finds that a fist fight is in progress and the classroom is in an uproar. The special officer (security officer) separates the two students who are fighting and takes them out of the room. Both of them seem to be intoxicated. They both have valid student ID cards.
   ACTION: The special officer (security officer) takes down their names and addresses for his report, then tells them to leave the building with a warning not to return this evening.

   The CORRECT answer is:

   A. I   B. II   C. III   D. IV

3. **GENERAL RULE**: A special officer (security officer) is not permitted to carry a gun while on duty.
   EXCEPTION: A special officer (security officer) who disarms a person must keep the weapon in his possession for the brief period before he can turn it over to the proper authorities. A special officer (security officer) who is NOT on duty may, like any other citizen, own and carry a gun if he has a proper permit from the Police Department.
   PROBLEM: A special officer (security officer) is assigned to a post where there have been a series of violent incidents in the past few days. He feels that these incidents could have been controlled much more easily if the people involved had seen that the special officer (security officer) had a gun. He has a gun at home, for which he has a valid permit.
   ACTION: The special officer (security officer) brings his gun when he goes on duty. He does not plan to use it, but just show people that he has it so that they will not start any trouble.

   The CORRECT answer is:

   A. I   B. II   C. III   D. IV

4. **GENERAL RULE**: No one except a licensed physician or someone acting directly under a physician's orders may legally administer medicine to another person.
   EXCEPTION: In a first aid situation, the special officer (security officer) is allowed to help a person suffering frori a heart condition or other disease to take medicine which the person has in his possession, provided that the person is conscious and requests this assistance.
   PROBLEM: A special officer (security officer) on duty at a public building is told that a man has collapsed in the elevator. When the special officer (security officer) arrives at the scene, the man is barely conscious. He cannot speak, but he points to his pocket. The special officer (security officer) finds a pill bottle that says *one capsule in ease of need*. The man nods.
   ACTION: The special officer (security officer) puts one capsule in the man's hand and guides the man's hand to his mouth.

   The CORRECT answer is:

   A. I   B. II   C. III   D. IV

5. **GENERAL RULE**: In case of a fire drill or fire alarm, special officers (security officers) on patrol in a building are to remain in their assigned areas to assist in the evacuation of persons from the building and to make sure that no one takes advantage of the situation by stealing property that is left unguarded.
   EXCEPTION: Should there be an actual fire, special officers (security officers) will follow whatever instructions are given by the firefighters or police officers who arrive on the scene to take charge.
   PROBLEM: A special officer (security officer) is on duty patroling the fifth floor of a building when a fire alarm sounds. The fire is in a supply closet at one end of the fifth floor. All personnel have been evacuated from the floor. Neither police nor firemen have yet shown up.
   ACTION: The special officer (security officer) stays on the fifth floor at a safe distance from the supply closet.

   The CORRECT answer is:

   A. I   B. II   C. III   D. IV

KEY (CORRECT ANSWERS)

1. B
2. A
3. D
4. B
5. A

EXAMINATION SECTION
TEST 1

DIRECTIONS: Each question or incomplete statement is followed by several suggested answers or completions. Select the one that BEST answers the question or completes the statement. *PRINT THE LETTER OF THE CORRECT ANSWER IN THE SPACE AT THE RIGHT.*

1. As a general rule, which of the following areas on a campus would be most in need of protection by a physical barrier?
Areas

    A. set aside for group activities
    B. smaller than 40 feet in diameter
    C. with roof access
    D. less than 18 feet above ground

    1.____

2. For a campus officer to be armed, it is customary for him to complete a signed statement pledging himself to certain guidelines. Which of the following would typically be included in such a statement?
    I. The firearm will never be used as a club or similar weapon.
    II. Before shooting directly at a person, the officer will fire at least one warning shot.
    III. The firearm is only to be drawn when the officer's life, or the life of another, is threatened.
    IV. Shots directed at a perpetrator should be intended to disable, rather than kill.
The CORRECT answer is:

    A. I, III
    B. I, III, IV
    C. III *only*
    D. II, III, IV

    2.____

3. An arrest that is made after the security officer sees the offense committed is known as an arrest on

    A. reasonable suspicion of probable cause
    B. view
    C. detention
    D. complaint

    3.____

4. The gate valve alarm of a sprinkler system has sounded. This means that the

    A. sprinkler system has been activated
    B. main water riser to the valve has been shut off
    C. storage water level has dropped below minimum requirements
    D. secondary water valve has been closed

    4.____

5. A *dry* fire — from burning wood, paper, or textiles — is classified as Class

    A. A   B. B   C. C   D. D

    5.____

6. The main DISADVANTAGE associated with the use of local alarms in security systems is that

   A. sometimes nobody is around to hear them
   B. they are dependent on electrical power
   C. they must be placed in multiple locations
   D. they don't deter criminals from breaking and entering

7. Each of the following is a symptom exhibited by *huffers* of vapors produced by glue, gasoline, paint, or other substances EXCEPT

   A. slurred speech
   B. violent behavior
   C. coughing
   D. increased appetite

8. Legally, a theft from the inside of a vehicle that has been locked and entered unlawfully is called

   A. robbery
   B. grand larceny
   C. burglary
   D. petty larceny

9. Security problems that may be caused by severe heat include

   A. increased likelihood of loss of power
   B. electrical overheating
   C. greater ability for people to hide stolen property
   D. increased likelihood of fires

10. Which of the following campus features does the most to necessitate a 24-hour radio dispatcher?
    A

    A. residential community
    B. contractual installation such as food service
    C. valuable collection
    D. high-rise building or buildings

11. If rounds clocks are used by an officer on patrol,

    A. the clock areas should be evenly spaced
    B. each clock must be punched on every round, regardless of the order
    C. the clock locations should never be changed
    D. they should be punched in exactly the same order each time

12. Because of the operating costs involved, a _____ alarm system is used primarily for government-owned facilities.

    A. remote
    B. central station
    C. local
    D. proprietary station

13. When assisting victims at the scene of an accident, an officer may
    I. give nonprescription medication
    II. restrain a person who is having a seizure
    III. treat a victim for shock
    IV. give the person fluids if the person is conscious
    The CORRECT answer is:

    A. I only
    B. II only
    C. III, IV
    D. IV only

14. When a(n) _____ is NOT generally an occasion on which a person, automobile, or premises may be legally searched.

    A. subject is being held for questioning
    B. warrant has been obtained
    C. emergency situation exists
    D. lawful arrest has been made

15. After a crime has been committed, a(n) _____ makes the most useful interview subject.

    A. witness   B. victim   C. suspect   D. informant

16. A _____ lock generally offers the LEAST amount of security.

    A. combination   B. pin tumbler
    C. disc tumbler   D. cipher

17. Evacuation guidelines for most campus buildings provide for an area warden, stair guard, and a group leader who is appointed from among the building's management personnel. Typically, a group leader will be responsible for controlling and directing about _____ people, depending on the floor size and layout.

    A. 5   B. 15   C. 25   D. 35

18. The campus has just received a bomb threat, and a search is underway. When searching individual rooms, an officer should begin

    A. at the door and move in a circular path
    B. at the corners and move inward
    C. with the furniture and then check the fixtures
    D. at the ceiling and move to the floor

19. The highest percentage of crime on school campuses typically occurs in

    A. classrooms and private offices
    B. residence hall or dorms
    C. parking lots
    D. commercial installations such as bookstores and food service

20. For most security applications, a report listing the holder of keys must be filed

    A. twice daily   B. daily
    C. twice weekly   D. weekly

21. The best driving speed for vehicle patrol services is generally between _____ miles per hour.

    A. 5-10   B. 15-20   C. 25-30   D. 35-40

22. Which of the following statements is generally FALSE?

    A. An officer should never approach a group of people without requesting backup, even if it is not needed.
    B. The officer should never draw a weapon as a tactic for discouraging violence.
    C. An officer should never confront hostile persons alone.
    D. When using a flashlight, the officer should hold it sheltered close to his body.

23. In general, security personnel may make an arrest if they
    I. observe a suspect taking property
    II. know a felony has been committed but did not see it happen
    III. know a misdemeanor has been committed but did not see it happen
    The CORRECT answer is:

    A. I only
    B. I, II
    C. I, III
    D. II, III

24. Which of the following may be a visible symptom of the abuse of opiates such as morphine, codeine, or heroin?

    A. Antisocial behavior
    B. Constricted eye functions
    C. Pale, sweaty skin
    D. Rapid speech

25. A security officer is the first to arrive at the scene of an accident that has caused injury. The victim has an open wound that is bleeding dark red, in a steady stream. After taking precautions against blood-borne disease, the officer should

    A. flush the wound with water
    B. apply a tourniquet
    C. apply antiseptic
    D. apply direct pressure to the wound

26. When approaching a subject for a weapons search, the officer should inform the subject that the search is to be conducted

    A. after the subject has been apprehended
    B. from behind, with one hand placed on the subject's shoulder
    C. from the patrol car, through a bullhorn or intercom
    D. from a safe distance of at least five feet

27. Which of the following elements should be included in a shift report?
    I. Detailed accounts of reported incidents
    II. Time and number of patrol rounds completed
    III. Information on condition of lighting
    IV. Weather conditions
    The CORRECT answer is:

    A. I only
    B. II, III, IV
    C. III, IV
    D. I, II

28. A(n) _____ internal alarm would probably be most effective in protecting a safe or vault.

    A. audio
    B. ultrasonic
    C. photoelectric
    D. capacitance

29. A call has come in from a passenger on a stranded elevator to the switchboard operator. After the operator receives the relevant information, security and maintenance personnel are contacted. Security personnel should report to the

    A. floor where the elevator is stranded
    B. maintenance personnel for direction
    C. bottom floor
    D. top floor

30. The post indicator alarm of a sprinkler system has sounded. This means the

    A. sprinkler system has been activated
    B. main water riser to the valve has been shut off
    C. storage water level has dropped below minimum requirements
    D. secondary water valve has been closed

31. The primary goal of a private security officer at the scene of a recent crime is

    A. containment
    B. witness interviews
    C. suspect apprehension
    D. evidence gathering

32. If a security officer encounters an accident victim who has gone into shock, the officer should do each of the following EXCEPT

    A. keep the victim warm
    B. raise the victim's head
    C. treat injuries
    D. loosen the victim's clothing

33. For a security officer, the foundation of good report writing is considered to be

    A. through patrolling
    B. good interviewing
    C. field note taking
    D. outlining skills

34. The fundamental difference between a crime called *malicious destruction of property* and one called *vandalism* is one of

    A. jurisdiction
    B. apparent motive
    C. the monetary amount of damage
    D. the type of property that was damaged

35. The most commonly used form of access control in setting such as college campuses is

    A. cipher locks
    B. compartmentalization
    C. flood lighting
    D. entry gate posts

36. The _____ should be allowed input into the decision to arm security personnel for specific situations or events.
    I. employers of security personnel
    II. public
    III. security agency
    IV. local law enforcement agency

    The CORRECT answer is:

    A. I, III
    B. I, IV
    C. II, III, IV
    D. II, IV

37. Which of the following activities generally offers the greatest degree of flexibility in the delivery of security services?

    A. Report writing
    B. Vehicle patrol
    C. Access control
    D. Foot patrol

38. Which of the following is NOT a security concern that is generally associated with flooding?

    A. Usefulness of parking areas
    B. Evacuation plans
    C. Bursting water pipes
    D. Looting

39. Which of the following is a use-of-force guideline for private security personnel?

    A. If equipment (such as a flashlight) is not designed for use as a weapon, it should never be used for that purpose.
    B. If necessary, use a weapon as a form of intimidation to forestall the necessity of having to use it.
    C. Saps or billyclubs should be displayed prominently on the officer's belt to discourage resistance.
    D. The officer should use whatever force is necessary to overcome perceived resistance.

40. An informant has come forward to offer information about a crime that has been committed on campus. The security officer believes it is important to understand the informant's motivation for coming forward.
    Generally, the officer should approach this subject

    A. at the beginning of the interview
    B. when the informant least expects it
    C. after the informant has given an account, but before the officer has asked any questions
    D. at the conclusion of the interview

KEY (CORRECT ANSWERS)

1.	D	11.	A	21.	B	31.	A
2.	A	12.	A	22.	D	32.	B
3.	B	13.	C	23.	B	33.	C
4.	D	14.	A	24.	B	34.	B
5.	A	15.	A	25.	D	35.	D
6.	A	16.	C	26.	D	36.	A
7.	D	17.	B	27.	B	37.	B
8.	C	18.	A	28.	D	38.	C
9.	D	19.	B	29.	A	39.	A
10.	A	20.	B	30.	B	40.	D

TEST 2

DIRECTIONS: Each question or incomplete statement is followed by several suggested answers or completions. Select the one that BEST answers the question or completes the statement. *PRINT THE LETTER OF THE CORRECT ANSWER IN THE SPACE AT THE RIGHT.*

1. The campus has just received a bomb threat, and a search is underway. When searching individual rooms, team members should be instructed to

    A. start the search in the center of the room and move outward from there
    B. search slowly, first searching the area from the floor to waist height
    C. place a marker on any suspicious looking item
    D. enter a room completely before beginning the search

2. When on a foot patrol assignment, an officer should

    A. turn the lights off whenever leaving a building
    B. stick to the shadows and avoid being seen
    C. observe the area to be patrolled before entering
    D. stick to the same pattern of patrolling

3. Chemical fires are classified as Class

    A. A   B. B   C. C   D. D

4. If campus security officers are to be armed, a _____ is typically most appropriate for their use.

    A. shotgun
    B. short-nosed .38-caliber revolver
    C. carbine
    D. long-nosed .357 magnum

5. Which of the following is NOT a guideline that should be followed by security personnel who are on foot patrol at night?

    A. Avoid being lit from the back
    B. View the area to be patrolled in advance, if possible
    C. When entering buildings and are moving from room to room, open doors as quietly as possible
    D. Keep the flashlight on thumb pressure only

6. Which of the following types of locks is most likely to be used with cabinets and desks?

    A. Combination lock   B. Disc tumbler lock
    C. Padlock   D. Cipher lock

7. When on patrol, security personnel have an obligation to report
    I. traffic patterns
    II. improper employee conduct
    III. observed hazards
    IV. poor housekeeping or maintenance practices

    The CORRECT answer is:

    A. I *only*   B. II, IV
    C. II, III, IV   D. III, IV

8. Towing policies for the enforcement of campus parking should include each of the following EXCEPT

    A. a contractual arrangement with a tow truck operator
    B. fines returnable to the local municipality, if possible
    C. the presence of a security officer at each towing incident
    D. a random pattern of towing that includes first-time offenders

9. Which of the following statements is generally TRUE?

    A. An officer should always display his badge prominently, especially when on night patrol.
    B. An officer should communicate with a dispatcher or other officers constantly while on duty.
    C. When approaching a vehicle, an officer should walk directly in front of the vehicle headlights.
    D. If a door has a window, an officer should look through it and examine the room before entering.

10. Which of the following is a sign that might be exhibited by a person who is on amphetamines or *uppers*?

    A. Loss of appetite
    B. Constricted pupils
    C. Rapid speech
    D. Uncontrolled laughing

11. Whenever possible, security policy guidelines for campus residence halls should include each of the following EXCEPT

    A. a periphery of high-intensity light around the exterior
    B. the use of interchangeable-core locking cylinders
    C. the use of only one main ground-floor entrance per building
    D. planting shrubs/trees outside first-floor rooms

12. An alarm system whose monitors are located in the main guard office is known as a _____ alarm system.

    A. remote
    B. central station
    C. local
    D. proprietary station

13. A security officer comes across a victim who has been badly burned. The officer should

    A. treat the victim for shock
    B. bandage the burn
    C. apply cold water to the burn
    D. apply an ointment or salve

14. Which of the following interview subjects typically presents a security officer with the least amount of difficulty?
    A(n)

    A. witness   B. victim   C. suspect   D. informant

15. Access control to any campus will be ineffective in any case if _____ are not provided.

    A. physical barriers
    B. weapons
    C. floodlights
    D. secure locks

16. Generally, security personnel may detain a person if
    I. it is known that the subject has information regarding a crime
    II. there is probable cause to believe the person has unlawfully taken property that can be recovered by holding the person for a reasonable period of time
    III. it is suspected that the person will commit a crime in the near future
    The CORRECT answer is:

    A. I, II   B. II only   C. III only   D. I, III

17. In general, departmental record control should place a _____ day limit on the time allotted for the removal of files from the office by security personnel.

    A. 1   B. 2-3   C. 5-7   D. 10-15

18. Keys to gates, buildings, and other secured equipment must generally be issued and returned by officers

    A. every day
    B. every week
    C. every month
    D. annually

19. A crime has just been committed and a security officer is the first to arrive at the scene. Before the police arrive, a handful of campus officials arrive and request to enter the crime scene.
    The best way to handle this is to

    A. keep them out by any means necessary
    B. request their cooperation in remaining outside the scene until the police have arrived
    C. refer them to the security supervisor
    D. defer to their wishes

20. Which of the following phrases has a different meaning from the others?

    A. Incident report
    B. Post journal
    C. Shift report
    D. Post log

21. In order to be effective, combination locks used for access control should have AT LEAST _____ numbers.

    A. 3   B. 4   C. 5   D. 6

22. The simplest, most effective, and trouble-free peripheral alarm system for low-risk applications would probably involve

    A. magnetic switches
    B. button switches
    C. metallic foil tape
    D. audio switches

23. During a bomb search, a suspicious-looking package is found. Security personnel should

    A. move the package to a secure location
    B. place the package in water
    C. prevent anyone from touching the package
    D. place a tag on the package

24. When assisting a victim at the scene of an accident, an officer may
    I. describe an injury to the victim
    II. lift an injured person to a sitting position
    III. try to remove a foreign object from the victim's eye
    IV. attempt to keep the victim warm

    The CORRECT answer is:

    A. I only   B. II, III   C. IV only   D. III, IV

25. Each of the following is a symptom of shock EXCEPT

    A. slow pulse   B. intense thirst
    C. dilated pupils   D. irregular breathing

26. When on vehicle patrol, an officer should

    A. park directly in front of the building to be inspected
    B. observe from a distance or in a drive-by before driving into an area
    C. use spotlights to meet inspection requirements
    D. keep all windows closed while driving

27. Which of the following is a guideline to be followed by security personnel who are required to testify in court?

    A. Avoid asking attorneys to repeat their questions
    B. Never use the phrase *I think*
    C. Answer all questions as completely as possible
    D. Avoid looking directly at the judge or jury

28. Of the following types of arrest, the one that is most troublesome for security officers to justify is one that is made on

    A. reasonable suspicion of probable cause
    B. view
    C. detention
    D. complaint

29. The primary DISADVANTAGE associated with the use of central station alarm monitors is that

    A. time is lost from the time the signal is received until personnel arrive at the alarm area
    B. they do not provide a link to outside law enforcement agencies
    C. intruders are tipped off that the alarm has been activated
    D. they do not pin down the exact location of the alarm site

30. When writing any report, a security officer should

    A. write in the third person
    B. make sure there is at least one copy made
    C. use a formal outline
    D. use as few words as possible

31. Generally, campus property such as audio-visual equipment and office machinery should be inventoried at LEAST

    A. monthly
    B. quarterly
    C. annually
    D. every two years

32. Security personnel who carry firearms should generally be required to requalify themselves at a firing range every

    A. 4 months   B. 6 months   C. year   D. two years

33. Which of the following campus building areas is generally LEAST likely to be used for the placement of a bomb?

    A. Elevator shafts
    B. Toilets
    C. Roofs
    D. Electrical panels

34. If padlocks are used in security systems, it is recommended that they be made of

    A. aluminum
    B. case-hardened steel
    C. cast iron
    D. hardened steel

35. An officer should make certain assumptions about foot patrol assignments. Which of the following is NOT one of these?

    A. Some form of communication is available for the officer to obtain assistance or request instructions.
    B. Most foot patrol assignments are single-officer duties.
    C. Only buildings that are open for public access will be included in the assignment.
    D. Back-up officers are available but are at some distance.

36. Which of the following statements about security personnel arrests is/are generally TRUE?
    I. The subject does not have to be under control in order for there to be an arrest.
    II. Detaining a person is a technical arrest.
    III. An arrest is made with the arresting persons identifying themselves and make a statement such as *you are under arrest,* and either touch the suspect or the suspect agrees.
    IV. The authority for the arrest must be known by the suspect.

    The CORRECT answer is:

    A. I, II, IV
    B. II, III, IV
    C. III, IV
    D. I, III

37. As a general rule, an area that is less than _____ from another structure should be protected by a physical barrier.

    A. 14 feet   B. 25 feet   C. 64 feet   D. 100 yards

38. Security concerns associated with extreme cold include each of the following EXCEPT

    A. delayed communication
    B. physical danger from frozen surfaces
    C. increased opportunity for concealing objects under clothes
    D. integrity of plumbing systems

39. Fires from flammable liquids or grease are classified as Class

    A. A B. B C. C D. D

40. When interviewing the victim of a crime, which of the following is a guideline that should generally be followed by a security officer?

    A. Make sure at least one other officer is present.
    B. Maintain a calm, steady demeanor.
    C. Get the facts by any means necessary.
    D. Keep the victim away from others who are familiar to him/her.

KEY (CORRECT ANSWERS)

1. B	11. D	21. B	31. C
2. C	12. D	22. A	32. A
3. D	13. A	23. C	33. C
4. B	14. D	24. C	34. D
5. C	15. A	25. A	35. C
6. B	16. B	26. B	36. B
7. C	17. B	27. B	37. A
8. D	18. A	28. A	38. A
9. B	19. B	29. A	39. B
10. C	20. A	30. B	40. B

EXAMINATION SECTION
TEST 1

DIRECTIONS: Each question or incomplete statement is followed by several suggested answers or completions. Select the one that BEST answers the question or completes the statement. *PRINT THE LETTER OF THE CORRECT ANSWER IN THE SPACE AT THE RIGHT.*

Questions 1-4.

DIRECTIONS: Questions 1 through 4 are based on the picture entitled *Contents of a Woman's Handbag*. Assume that all of the contents are shown in the picture.

CONTENTS OF A WOMAN'S HANDBAG

1. Where does Gladys Constantine live?

    A. Chalmers Street in Manhattan
    B. Summer Street in Manhattan
    C. Summer Street in Brooklyn
    D. Chalmers Street in Brooklyn

2. How many keys were in the handbag?

    A. 2   B. 3   C. 4   D. 5

3. How much money was in the handbag? _____ dollar(s).

    A. Exactly five   B. More than five
    C. Exactly ten   D. Less than one

4. The sales slip found in the handbag shows the purchase of which of the following?

    A. The handbag   B. Lipstick
    C. Tissues   D. Prescription medicine

Questions 5-8.

DIRECTIONS: Questions 5 through 8 are based on the floor plan below.

FLOOR PLAN

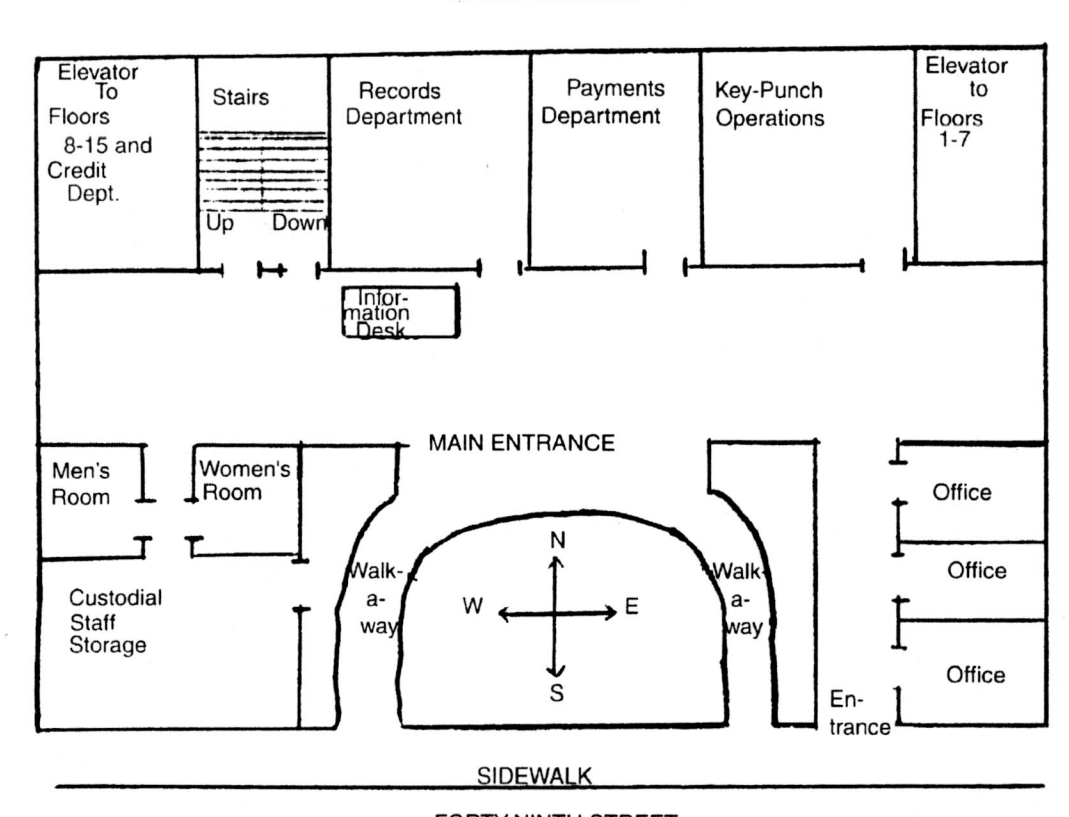

5. A special officer (security officer) on duty at the main entrance must be aware of other outside entrances to his area of the building. These unguarded entrances are usually kept locked, but they are important in case of fire or other emergency.
Besides the main entrance, how many OTHER entrances shown on the floor plan directly face Forty-ninth Street?
_____ other entrances.

   A. No   B. One   C. Two   D. Three

   5.____

6. A person who arrives at the main entrance and asks to be directed to the Credit Department SHOULD be told to

   A. take the elevator on the left
   B. take the elevator on the right
   C. go to a different entrance
   D. go up the stairs on the left

   6.____

7. On the east side of the entrance can be found

   A. a storage room   B. offices
   C. toilets   D. stairs

   7.____

8. The space DIRECTLY BEHIND the Information Desk in the floor plan is occupied by

   A. up and down stairs   B. key punch operations
   C. toilets   D. the records department

   8.____

Questions 9-12.

DIRECTIONS: Answer Questions 9 to 12 on the basis of the information given in the passage below.

The public often believes that the main job of a uniformed officer is to enforce laws by simply arresting people. In reality, however, many of the situations that an officer deals with do not call for the use of his arrest power. In the first place, an officer spends much of his time <u>preventing</u> crimes from happening, by spotting potential violations or suspicious behavior and taking action to prevent illegal acts. In the second place, many of the situations in which officers are called on for assistance involve elements like personal arguments, husband-wife quarrels, noisy juveniles, or mentally disturbed persons. The majority of these problems do not result in arrests and convictions, and often they do not even involve illegal behavior. In the third place, even in situations where there seems to be good reason to make an arrest, an officer may have to exercise very good judgment. There are times when making an arrest too soon could touch off a riot, or could result in the detention of a minor offender while major offenders escaped, or could cut short the gathering of necessary on-the-scene evidence.

9. The above passage IMPLIES that most citizens

   A. will start to riot if they see an arrest being made
   B. appreciate the work that law enforcement officers do
   C. do not realize that making arrests is only a small part of law enforcement
   D. never call for assistance unless they are involved in a personal argument or a husband-wife quarrel

   9.____

10. According to the passage, one way in which law enforcement officers can prevent crimes from happening is by

    A. arresting suspicious characters
    B. letting minor offenders go free
    C. taking action on potential violations
    D. refusing to get involved in husband-wife fights

11. According to the passage, which of the following statements is NOT true of situations involving mentally disturbed persons?

    A. It is a waste of time to call on law enforcement officers for assistance in such situations.
    B. Such situations may not involve illegal behavior
    C. Such situations often do not result in arrests.
    D. Citizens often turn to law enforcement officers for help in such situations.

12. The last sentence in the passage mentions *detention of minor offenders*.
    Of the following, which BEST explains the meaning of the word *detention* as used here?

    A. Sentencing someone
    B. Indicting someone
    C. Calling someone before a grand jury
    D. Arresting someone

Questions 13-28.

DIRECTIONS: In answering Questions 13 through 28, assume that *you* means a special officer (security officer) on duty. Your basic responsibilities are safeguarding people and property and maintaining order in the area to which you are assigned. You are in uniform, and you are not armed. You keep in touch with your supervisory station either by telephone or by a two-way radio (walkie-talkie).

13. It is a general rule that if the security alarm goes off showing that someone has made an unlawful entrance into a building, no officer responsible for security shall proceed to investigate alone. Each officer must be accompanied by at least one other officer.
    Of the following, which is the MOST probable reason for this rule?

    A. It is dangerous for an officer to investigate such a situation alone.
    B. The intruder might try to bribe an officer to let him go.
    C. One officer may be inexperienced and needs an experienced partner.
    D. Two officers are better than one officer in writing a report of the investigation.

14. You are on weekend duty on the main floor of a public building. The building is closed to the public on weekends, but some employees are sometimes asked to work weekends. You have been instructed to use cautious good judgment in opening the door for such persons.
    Of the following, which one MOST clearly shows the poorest judgment?

A. Admitting an employee who is personally known to you without asking to see any identification except the permit slip signed by the employee's supervisor
B. Refusing to admit someone whom you do not recognize but who claims left his identification at home
C. Admitting to the building only those who can give a detailed description of their weekend work duties
D. Leaving the entrance door locked for a while to make regulation security checks of other areas in the building with the result that no one can either enter or leave during these periods

15. You are on duty at a public building. An office employee tells you that she left her purse in her desk when she went out to lunch, and she has just discovered that it is gone. She has been back from lunch for half an hour and has not left her desk during this period. What should you do FIRST? 15.____

    A. Warn all security personnel to stop any suspicious-looking person who is seen with a purse
    B. Ask for a description of the purse
    C. Call the Lost and Found and ask if a purse has been turned in
    D. Obtain statements from any employees who were in the office during the lunch hour

16. You are patrolling your assigned area in a public building. You hear a sudden crash and the sound of running footsteps. You investigate and find that someone has forced open a locked entrance to the building. What is the FIRST thing you should do? 16.____

    A. Close the door and try to fix the lock so that no one else can get in
    B. Use your two-way radio to report the emergency and summon help
    C. Chase after the person whose running footsteps you heard
    D. Go immediately to your base office and make out a brief written report

17. You and another special officer (security officer) are on duty in the main waiting area at a welfare center. A caseworker calls both of you over and whispers that one of the clients, Richard Roe, may be carrying a gun. Of the following, what is the BEST action for both of you to take? 17.____

    A. You should approach the man, one on each side, and one of you should say loudly and clearly, *"Richard Roe, you are under arrest."*
    B. Both of you should ask the man to go with you to a private room, and then find out if he is carrying a gun
    C. Both of you should grab him, handcuff him, and take him to the nearest precinct station house
    D. Both of you should watch him carefully but not do anything unless he actually pulls a gun

18. You are on duty at a welfare center. You are told that a caseworker is being threatened by a man with a knife. You go immediately to the scene, and you find the caseworker lying on the floor with blood spurting from a wound in his arm. You do not know who the attacker is. What should you do FIRST? 18.____

    A. Ask the caseworker for a description of the attacker so that you can set out in pursuit and try to catch him
    B. Take down the names and addresses of any witnesses to the incident

C. Give first aid to the caseworker, if you can, and immediately call for an ambulance
D. Search the people standing around in the room for the knife

19. As a special officer (security officer), you have been patrolling a special section of a hospital building for a week. Smoking is not allowed in this section because the oxygen tanks in use here could easily explode. However, you have observed that some employees sneak into the linen-supply room in this section in order to smoke without anybody seeing them.
Of the following, which is the BEST way for you to deal with this situation?

    A. Whenever you catch anyone smoking, call his supervisor immediately
    B. Request the Building Superintendent to put a padlock on the door of the linen-supply room
    C. Ignore the smoking because you do not want to get a reputation for interfering in the private affairs of other employees
    D. Report the situation to your supervisor and follow his instructions

20. You are on duty at a hospital. You have been assigned to guard the main door, and you are responsible for remaining at your post until relieved. On one of the wards for which you are not responsible, there is a patient who was wounded in a street fight. This patient is under arrest for killing another man in this fight, and he is supposed to be under round-the-clock police guard. A nurse tells you that one of the police officers assigned to guard the patient has suddenly taken ill and has to periodically leave his post to go to the washroom. The nurse is worried because she thinks the patient might try to escape.
Of the following, which is the BEST action for you to take?

    A. Tell the nurse to call you whenever the police officer leaves his post so that you can keep an eye on the patient while the officer is gone
    B. Assume that the police officer probably knows his job, and that there is no reason for you to worry
    C. Alert your supervisor to the nurse's report
    D. Warn the police officer that the nurse has been talking about him

21. You are on night duty at a hospital where you are responsible for patrolling a large section of the main building. Your supervisor tells you that there have been several nighttime thefts from a supply room in your section and asks you to be especially alert for suspicious activity near this supply room.
Of the following, which is the MOST reasonable way to carry out your supervisor's direction?

    A. Check the supply room regularly at half-hour intervals
    B. Make frequent checks of the supply room at irregular intervals
    C. Station yourself by the door of the supply room and stay at this post all night
    D. Find a hidden spot from which you can watch the supply room and stay there all night

22. You are on duty at a vehicle entrance to a hospital. Parking space on the hospital grounds is strictly limited, and no one is ever allowed to park there unless they have an official parking permit. You have just stopped a driver who does not have a parking permit, but he explains that
he is a doctor and he has a patient in the hospital. What should you do?

A. Let him park since he has explained that he is a doctor
B. Ask in a friendly way, *"Can I check your identification?"*
C. Call the Information Desk to make sure there is such a patient in the hospital
D. Tell the driver politely but firmly that he will have to park somewhere else

23. You are on duty at a public building. A man was just mugged on a stairway. The mugger took the man's wallet and started to run down the stairs but tripped and fell. Now the mugger is lying unconscious at the bottom of the stairs and bleeding from the mouth.
The FIRST thing you should do is to

    A. search him to see if he is carrying any other stolen property
    B. pick him up and carry him away from the stairs
    C. try and revive him for questioning
    D. put in a call for an ambulance and police assistance

24. After someone breaks into an employee's locker at a public building, you interview the employee to determine what is missing from the locker. The employee becomes hysterical and asks why you are *wasting time with all these questions* instead of going after the thief.
The MOST reasonable thing for you to do is

    A. tell the employee that it is very important to have an accurate description of the missing articles
    B. quietly tell the employee to calm down and stop interfering with your work
    C. explain to the employee that you are only doing what you were told to do and that you don't make the rules
    D. assure the employee that there are a lot of people working on the case and that someone else is probably arresting the thief right now

25. You are on duty at a public building. An employee reports that a man has just held her up and taken her money. The employee says that the man was about 25 years old, with short blond hair and a pale complexion and was wearing blue jeans.
Of the following additional facts, which one would probably be MOST valuable to officers searching the building for the suspect?

    A. The man was wearing dark glasses.
    B. He had on a green jacket.
    C. He was about 5 feet 8 inches tall.
    D. His hands and fingernails were very dirty.

26. When the fire alarm goes off, it is your job as a special officer (security officer) to see that all employees leave the building quickly by the correct exits. A fire alarm has just sounded, and you are checking the offices on one of the floors. A supervisor in one office tells you, *"This is probably just another fire drill. I've sent my office staff out, but I don't want to stop my own work."*
What should you do?

    A. Insist politely but firmly that the supervisor must obey the fire rules.
    B. Tell the supervisor that it is all right this time but that the rules must be followed in the future.
    C. Tell the supervisor that he is under arrest.
    D. Allow the supervisor to do as he sees fit since he is in charge of his own office.

27. You are on duty on the main floor of a public building. You have been informed that a briefcase has just been stolen from an office on the tenth floor. You see a man getting off the elevator with a briefcase that matches the description of the one that was stolen.
What is the FIRST action you should take?

   A. Arrest the man and take him to the nearest public station
   B. Stop the man and say politely that you want to take a look at the briefcase
   C. Take the briefcase from the man and tell him that he cannot have it back unless he can prove that it is his
   D. Do not stop the man but note down his description and the exact time he got off the elevator

27.____

28. You are on duty at a welfare center. You have been told that two clients are arguing with a caseworker and making loud threats. You go to the scene, but the caseworker tells you that everything is now under control. The two clients, who are both mean-looking characters, are still there but seem to be acting normally.
What SHOULD you do?

   A. Apologize for having made a mistake and go away.
   B. Arrest the two men for having caused a disturbance.
   C. Insist on standing by until the interview is over, then escort the two men from the building.
   D. Leave the immediate scene but watch for any further developments.

28.____

29. You are on duty at a welfare center. A client comes up to you and says that two men just threatened him with a knife and made him give them his money. The client has alcohol on his breath and he is shabbily dressed. He points out the two men he says took the money.
Of the following, which is the BEST action to take?

   A. Arrest the two men on the client's complaint.
   B. Ignore the client's complaint since he doesn't look as if he could have had any money.
   C. Suggest to the client that he may be imagining things.
   D. Investigate and find out what happened.

29.____

Questions 30-35.

DIRECTIONS: Answer Questions 30 through 35 on the basis of the information given in the passage below. Assume that all questions refer to the same state described in the passage.

The courts and the police consider an "offense" as any conduct that is punishable by a fine or imprisonment. Such offenses include many kinds of acts - from behavior that is merely annoying, like throwing a noisy party that keeps everyone awake, all the way up to violent acts like murder. The law classifies offenses according to the penalties that are provided for them. In one state, minor offenses are called "violations." A violation is punishable by a fine of not more than $250 or imprisonment of not more than 15 days, or both. The annoying behavior mentioned above is an example of a violation. More serious offenses are classified as "crimes." Crimes are classified by the kind of penalty that is provided. A "misdemeanor" is a crime that is punishable by a fine of not more than $1,000 or by imprisonment of not more than one year, or both. Examples of misdemeanors include stealing something with a value *of $100 or less, turning in a false alarm, or illegally possessing less than 1/8 of an ounce of a dangerous drug. A "felony" is a criminal offense punishable by imprisonment of more than one year. Murder is clearly a felony.*

30. According to the above passage, any act that is punishable by imprisonment or by a fine is called a(n)   30._____

    A. offense   B. violation   C. crime   D. felony

31. According to the above passage, which of the following is classified as a crime?   31._____

    A. Offense punishable by 15 days imprisonment
    B. Minor offense
    C. Violation
    D. Misdemeanor

32. According to the above passage, if a person guilty of burglary can receive a prison sentence of 7 years or more, burglary would be classified as a   32._____

    A. violation   B. misdemeanor
    C. felony   D. violent act

33. According to the above passage, two offenses that would BOTH be classified as misdemeanors are   33._____

    A. making unreasonable noise and stealing a $90 bicycle
    B. stealing a $75 radio and possessing 1/16 of an ounce of heroin
    C. holding up a bank and possessing 1/4 of a pound of marijuana
    D. falsely reporting a fire and illegally double-parking

34. The above passage says that offenses are classified according to the penalties provided for them.
    On the basis of clues in the passage, who probably decides what the maximum penalties should be for the different kinds of offenses?   34._____

    A. The State lawmakers   B. The City police
    C. The Mayor   D. Officials in Washington, B.C.

35. Of the following, which BEST describes the subject matter of the passage?   35._____

    A. How society deals with criminals
    B. How offenses are classified
    C. Three types of criminal behavior
    D. The police approach to offenders

KEY (CORRECT ANSWERS)

1.	C	16.	B
2.	C	17.	B
3.	B	18.	C
4.	D	19.	D
5.	B	20.	C
6.	A	21.	B
7.	B	22.	D
8.	D	23.	D
9.	C	24.	A
10.	C	25.	C
11.	A	26.	A
12.	D	27.	B
13.	A	28.	D
14.	C	29.	D
15.	B	30.	A

31. D
32. C
33. B
34. A
35. B

TEST 2

DIRECTIONS: Each question or incomplete statement is followed by several suggested answers or completions. Select the one that BEST answers the question or completes the statement. *PRINT THE LETTER OF THE CORRECT ANSWER IN THE SPACE AT THE RIGHT.*

Questions 1-5.

DIRECTIONS: Questions 1 through 5 are based on the drawing below showing a view of a waiting area in a public building.

1. A desk is shown in the drawing. Which of the following is on the desk? A(n)   1._____
    A. plant
    B. telephone
    C. In-Out file
    D. *Information* sign

2. On which floor is the waiting area?

   A. Basement
   B. Main floor
   C. Second floor
   D. Third floor

3. The door IMMEDIATELY TO THE RIGHT of the desk is a(n)

   A. door to the Personnel Office
   B. elevator door
   C. door to another corridor
   D. door to the stairs

4. Among the magazines on the tables in the waiting area are

   A. TIME and NEWSWEEK
   B. READER'S DIGEST and T.V. GUIDE
   C. NEW YORK and READER'S DIGEST
   D. TIME and T.V. GUIDE

5. One door is partly open. This is the door to

   A. the Director's office
   B. the Personnel Manager's office
   C. the stairs
   D. an unmarked office

Questions 6-9.

DIRECTIONS: Questions 6 through 9 are based on the drawing below showing the contents of a male suspect's pockets.

CONTENTS OF A MALE SUSPECT'S POCKETS

6. The suspect had a slip in his pockets showing an appointment at an out-patient clinic on 6.____

   A. February 9, 2013 B. September 2, 2013
   C. February 19, 2013 D. September 12, 2013

7. The MP3 player that was found on the suspect was made by 7.____

   A. RCA B. GE C. Sony D. Zenith

8. The coins found in the suspect's pockets have a TOTAL value of 8.____

   A. 56¢ B. 77¢ C. $1.05 D. $1.26

9. All except one of the following were found in the suspect's pockets. 9.____
   Which was NOT found? A

   A. ticket stub B. comb
   C. subway fare D. pen

Questions 10-18

DIRECTIONS: In answering Questions 10 through 18, assume that *you* means a special officer (security officer) on duty. Your basic responsibilities are safeguarding people and property and maintaining order in the area to which you are assigned. You are in uniform, and you are not armed. You keep in touch with your supervisory station either by telephone or by a two-way radio (a walkie-talkie).

10. You are on duty at a center run by the Department of Social Services. Two teenaged 10.____
    boys are on their way out of the center. As they go past you, they look at you and laugh, and one makes a remark to you in Spanish. You do not understand Spanish, but you suspect it was a nasty remark.
    What SHOULD you do?

    A. Give the boys a lecture about showing respect for a uniform.
    B. Tell the boys that they had better stay away from the center from now on.
    C. Call for an interpreter and insist that the boy repeat the remark to the interpreter.
    D. Let the boys go on their way since they have done nothing requiring your intervention.

11. You are on duty at a shelter run by the Department of Social Services. You know that 11.____
    many of the shelter clients have drinking problems, drug problems, or mental health problems. You get a call for assistance from a caseworker who says a fight has broken out. When you arrive on the scene, you see that about a dozen clients are engaged in a free-for-all and that two or three of them have pulled knives.
    The BEST course of action is to

    A. call for additional assistance and order all bystanders away from the area
    B. jump into the center of the fighting group and try to separate the fighters
    C. pick up a heavy object and start swinging at anybody who has a knife
    D. try to find out what clients started the fight and place them under arrest

12. You have been assigned to duty at a children's shelter run by the Department of Social Services. The children range in age from 6 to 15, and many of them are at the shelter because they have no homes to go to.
Of the following, which is the BEST attitude for you to take in dealing with these youngsters?

    A. Assume that they admire and respect anyone in uniform and that they will not usually give you much trouble
    B. Assume that they fear and distrust anyone in uniform and that they are going to give you a hard time unless you act tough
    C. Expect that many of them are going to become juvenile delinquents because of their bad backgrounds and that you should be suspicious of everything they do
    D. Expect that many of them may be emotionally upset and that you should be alert for unusual behavior

13. You are on duty outside the emergency room of a hospital. You notice that an old man has been sitting on a bench outside the room for a long time. He arrived alone, and he has not spoken to anyone at all.
What SHOULD you do?

    A. Pay no attention to him since he is not bothering anyone.
    B. Tell him to leave since he does not seem to have any business there.
    C. Ask him if you can help him in any way.
    D. Do not speak to him, but keep an eye on him.

14. You are patrolling a section of a public building. An elderly woman carrying a heavy shopping bag asks you if you would watch the shopping bag for her while she keeps an appointment in the building.
What SHOULD you do?

    A. Watch the shopping bag for her since her appointment probably will not take long.
    B. Refuse her request, explaining that your duties keep you on the move.
    C. Agree to her request just to be polite, but then continue your patrol after the woman is out of sight.
    D. Find a bystander who will agree to watch the shopping bag for her.

15. You are on duty at a public building. It is nearly 6:00 P.M., and most employees have left for the day.
You see two well-dressed men carrying an office calculating machine out of the building. You SHOULD

    A. stop them and ask for an explanation
    B. follow them to see where they are going
    C. order them to put down the machine and leave the building immediately
    D. take no action since they do not look like burglars

16. You are on duty patrolling a public building. You have just tripped on the stairs and turned your ankle. The ankle hurts and is starting to swell.
What is the BEST thing to do?

A. Take a taxi to a hospital emergency room, and from there have a hospital employee call your supervisor to explain the situation.
B. First try soaking your foot in cold water for half an hour, then go off duty if you really cannot walk at all.
C. Report the situation to your supervisor, explaining that you need prompt medical attention for your ankle.
D. Find a place where you can sit until you are due to go off duty, then have a doctor look at your ankle.

17. One of your duties as a special officer (security officer) on night patrol in a public building is to check the washrooms to see that the taps are turned off and that there are no plumbing leaks.
Of the following possible reasons for this inspection, which is probably the MOST important reason? 17.____

A. If the floor gets wet, someone might slip and fall the next morning.
B. A running water tap might be a sign that there is an intruder in the building.
C. A washroom flood could leak through the ceilings and walls below and cause a lot of damage.
D. Leaks must be reported quickly so that repairs can be scheduled as soon as possible.

18. You are on duty at a public building. A department supervisor tells you that someone has left a suspicious-looking package in the hallway on his floor. You investigate, and you hear ticking in the parcel. You think it could be a bomb.
The FIRST thing you should do is to 18.____

A. rapidly question employees on this floor to get a description of the person who left the package
B. write down the description of the package and the name of the department supervisor
C. notify your security headquarters that there may be a bomb in the building and that all personnel should be evacuated
D. pick up the package carefully and remove it from the building as quickly as you can

Questions 19-22.

DIRECTIONS: Answer Questions 19 through 22 on the basis of the Fact Situation and the Report of Arrest form below. Questions 19 through 22 ask how the report form should be filled in based on the information given in the Fact Situation.

FACT SITUATION

Jesse Stein is a special officer (security officer) who is assigned to a welfare center at 435 East Smythe Street, Brooklyn. He was on duty there Thursday morning, February 1. At 10:30 A.M., a client named Jo Ann Jones, 40 years old, arrived with her ten-year-old son, Peter. Another client, Mary Alice Wiell, 45 years old, immediately began to insult Mrs. Jones. When Mrs. Jones told her to "go away," Mrs. Wiell pulled out a long knife. The special officer (security officer) intervened and requested Mrs. Wiell to drop the knife. She would not, and he had to use necessary force to disarm her. He arrested her on charges of disorderly conduct, harassment, and possession of a dangerous weapon. Mrs. Wiell lives at 118 Heally Street,

Brooklyn, Apartment 4F, and she is unemployed. The reason for her aggressive behavior is not known.

```
┌─────────────────────────────────────────────────────────────────────────┐
│ REPORT OF ARREST                                                        │
│                                                                         │
│ 01) _____   (08) _____  │
│     (Prisoner's surname)  (first)  (initial)       (Precinct)           │
│                                                                         │
│ 02) _____   (09) _____  │
│     (Address)                                      (Date of arrest)     │
│                                                    (Month, Day)         │
│                                                                         │
│ 03) _____ (04) _____ (05) _____  (10) _____ │
│     (Date of birth)   (Age)         (Sex)          (Time of arrest)     │
│                                                                         │
│ 06) _____ (07) _____  (11) _____ │
│     (Occupation)         (Where employed)          (Place of arrest)    │
│                                                                         │
│ 12) _____ │
│     (Specific offenses)                                                 │
│                                                                         │
│ 13) _____  (14) _____ │
│     (Arresting Officer)                        (Officer's No.)          │
└─────────────────────────────────────────────────────────────────────────┘
```

19. What entry should be made in Blank 01?

    A. Jo Ann Jones   B. Jones, Jo Ann
    C. Mary Wiell   D. Wiell, Mary A.

20. Which of the following should be entered in Blank 04?

    A. 40   B. 40's   C. 45   D. Middle-aged

21. Which of the following should be entered in Blank 09?

    A. Wednesday, February 1, 10:30 A.M.
    B. February 1
    C. Thursday morning, February 2
    D. Morning, February 4

22. Of the following, which would be the BEST entry to make in Blank 11?

    A. Really Street Welfare Center
    B. Brooklyn
    C. 435 E. Smythe St., Brooklyn
    D. 118 Healy St., Apt. 4F

Questions 23-27.

DIRECTIONS: Answer Questions 23 through 27 on the basis of the information given in the Report of Loss or Theft that appears below.

```
REPORT OF LOSS OR THEFT          Date: 12/4     Time: 9:15 a.m.
Complaint made by: Richard Aldridge          ☐ Owner
                   306 S. Walter St.          ☒ Other - explain:
                                              Head of Acctg. Dept.

Type of property: Computer                    Value: $550.00
Description: Dell
Location: 768 N Margin Ave., Accounting Dept., 3rd Floor
Time: Overnight 12/3 - 12/4
Circumstances: Mr. Aldridge reports he arrived at work 8:45 A.M.,
found office door open and machine missing. Nothing else reported
missing. I investigated and found signs of forced entry: door lock
was broken.          Signature of Reporting Officer: B.L. Ramirez

Notify:
  ☐ Building & Grounds Office, 768 N. Margin Ave.
  ☐ Lost Property Office, 110 Brand Ave.
  ☒ Security Office, 703 N. Wide Street
```

23. The person who made this complaint is

    A. a secretary
    B. a security officer
    C. Richard Aldridge
    D. B.L. Ramirez

24. The report concerns a computer that has been

    A. lost B. damaged C. stolen D. sold

25. The person who took the computer probably entered the office through

    A. a door B. a window C. the roof D. the basement

26. When did the head of the Accounting Department first notice that the computer was missing?

    A. December 4 at 9:15 A.M.
    B. December 4 at 8:45 A.M.
    C. The night of December 3
    D. The night of December 4

27. The event described in the report took place at

    A. 306 South Walter Street
    B. 768 North Margin Avenue
    C. 110 Brand Avenue
    D. 703 North Wide Street

8 (#2)

Questions 28-33.

DIRECTIONS: Answer Questions 28 through 33 on the basis of the instructions, the code, and the sample question given below.

Assume that a special officer (security officer) at a certain location is equipped with a two-way radio to keep him in constant touch with his security headquarters. Radio messages and replies are given in code form, as follows:

Radio Code for Situation	J	P	M	F	B
Radio Code for Action to be Taken	o	r	a	z	q
Radio Response for Action Being Taken	1	2	3	4	5

Assume that each of the above capital letters is the radio code for a particular type of situation, that the small letter below each capital letter is the radio code for the action a special officer (security officer) is directed to take, and that the number directly below each small letter is the radio response a special officer (security officer) should make to indicate what action was actually taken.

In each of the following Questions 28 through 33, the code letter for the action directed (Column 2) and the code number for the action taken (Column 3) should correspond to the capital letters in Column 1.

If only Column 2 is different from Column 1, mark your answer A.

If only Column 3 is different from Column 1, mark your answer B.

If both Column 2 and Column 3 are different from Column 1, mark your answer C.

If both Columns 2 and 3 are the same as Column 1, mark your answer D.

SAMPLE QUESTION

Column I	Column 2	Column 3
JPFMB	orzaq	12453

The code letters in Column 2 are correct, but the numbers 53 in Column 3 should be 35. Therefore, the answer is B.

	Column 1	Column 2	Column 3	
28.	PBFJM	rqzoa	25413	28.___
29.	MPFBJ	zrqao	32541	29.___
30.	JBFPM	oqzra	15432	30.___
31.	BJPMF	qaroz	51234	31.___
32.	PJFMB	rozaq	21435	32.___
33.	FJBMP	zoqra	41532	33.___

Questions 34-40.

DIRECTIONS: Questions 34 through 40 are based on the instructions given below. Study the instructions and the sample question; then answer Questions 34 through 40 on the basis of this information

INSTRUCTIONS:

In each of the following Questions 34 through 40, the 3-line name and address in Column 1 is the master-list entry, and the 3-line entry in Column 2 is the information to be checked against the master list.

If there is one line that does not match, mark your answer A.

If there are two lines that do not match, mark your answer B.

If all three lines do not match, mark your answer C.

If the lines all match exactly, mark your answer D.

SAMPLE QUESTION:

Column 1
Mark L. Field
11-09 Prince Park Blvd.
Bronx, N.Y. 11402

Column 2
Mark L. Field
11-99 Prince Park
Bronx, N.Y. 11401

The first lines in each column match exactly. The second lines do not match, since 11-09 does not match 11-99 and Blvd. does not match Way. The third lines do not match either, since 11402 does not match 11401. Therefore, there are two lines that do not match and the correct answer is B.

	Column 1	Column 2	
34.	Jerome A. Jackson 1243 14th Avenue New York, N.Y. 10023	Jerome A. Johnson 1234 14th Avenue New York, N.Y. 10023	34.____
35.	Sophie Strachtheim 33-28 Connecticut Ave. Far Rockaway, N.Y. 11697	Sophie Strachtheim 33-28 Connecticut Ave. Far Rockaway, N.Y. 11697	35.____
36.	Elisabeth N.T. Gorrell 256 Exchange St. New York, N.Y. 10013	Elizabeth N.T. Gorrell 256 Exchange St. New York, N.Y. 10013	36.____
37.	Maria J. Gonzalez 7516 E. Sheepshead Rd. Brooklyn, N.Y. 11240	Maria J. Gonzalez 7516 N. Shepshead Rd. Brooklyn, N.Y. 11240	37.____
38.	Leslie B. Brautenweiler 21 57A Seller Terr. Flushing, N.Y. 11367	Leslie B. Brautenwieler 21-75A Seiler Terr. Flushing, N.J. 11367	38.____

39. Rigoberto J. Peredes Rigoberto J. Peredes 39.____
    157 Twin Towers, #18F 157 Twin Towers, #18F
    Tottenville, S.I., N.Y. Tottenville, S.I., N.Y.

40. Pietro F. Albino Pietro F. Albina 40.____
    P.O. Box 7548 P.O. Box 7458
    Floral Park, N.Y. 11005 Floral Park, N.Y. 11005

KEY (CORRECT ANSWERS)

1. D	11. A	21. B	31. A
2. C	12. D	22. C	32. D
3. B	13. C	23. C	33. A
4. D	14. B	24. C	34. B
5. B	15. A	25. A	35. D
6. A	16. C	26. B	36. A
7. C	17. C	27. B	37. A
8. D	18. C	28. D	38. C
9. D	19. D	29. C	39. D
10. D	20. C	30. B	40. B

EXAMINATION SECTION
TEST 1

DIRECTIONS: Each question or incomplete statement is followed by several suggested answers or completions. Select the one that BEST answers the question or completes the statement. PRINT THE LETTER OF THE CORRECT ANSWER IN THE SPACE AT THE RIGHT.

1. When a security officer fails to report to work in time to make his scheduled relief, the security officer on duty must call the foreman immediately.
   The MAIN reason for this procedure is to

   A. make sure that the security officer on duty is not overworked
   B. make a record of the number of times that a security officer is late
   C. make sure that Authority property and materials are continuously guarded
   D. prevent the security officer who is late from being paid for the time that he did not work

2. A security officer must report to his foreman any employee who is on Authority property in an intoxicated condition.
   The MAIN reason for this procedure is that

   A. this employee may give the general public the impression that many Authority employees drink while on duty
   B. an employee who drinks on the job may encourage fellow employees to also drink on the job
   C. an intoxicated employee may endanger himself and other Authority employees
   D. the intoxicated employee's foreman may not have noticed this condition

3. If a security officer is required to make hourly calls to his foreman within twenty minutes of the hour, a correct time for a security officer to make his hourly call is at

   A. 3:36 A.M.   B. 8:29 A.M.   C. 4:27 A.M.   D. 7:48 P.M.

4. Which of the following characteristics of a security officer doing record keeping is MOST important?

   A. Familiarity with rules and procedures
   B. An analytical mind
   C. Accuracy
   D. Speed

5. Of the following, the type of equipment that a security officer working a 12:00 midnight to 8:00 A.M. shift would be expected to use MOST often is a

   A. pistol   B. flashlight   C. camera   D. siren

6. Before going on duty, a security officer is required to read all new bulletins posted on the bulletin board. The MAIN reason for this requirement is to

   A. acquaint the security officer with new regulations
   B. make sure that the security officer understands all the rules
   C. make the security officer responsible for any violations of the rules
   D. acquaint the security officer with his rights

7. Assume that soon after being appointed as a security officer, you decide that some of the rules and regulations of the Authority are unwise.
   Of the following, you should

   A. disregard these rules and regulations and use your own good judgment
   B. not do your job until some changes are made
   C. make the changes that you decide are necessary
   D. carry out these rules and regulations regardless of your opinion

Questions 8-11.
DIRECTIONS: Questions 8 to 11 are based on information contained in LOCATION OF KEY STATIONS shown below. When answering these questions, refer to this information.

LOCATION OF KEY STATIONS

No. 12 key station - located on double fire exit door adjacent to Briarcliff Avenue vehicle ramp.
No. 13 key station - located on wall adjacent to fire exit door in Unit Repair Section.
No. 14 key station - located in men's locker room on door leading to washroom near water cooler.
No. 15 key station - located in corridor leading to transportation area on wall adjacent to room number 1 and opposite to first aid room.
No. 16 key station - located on wall adjacent to door leading into unit storeroom.
No. 17 key station - located on a wall adjacent to double fire exit doors in Unit Repair Section.
No. 18 key station - located on wall adjacent to fire exit door in body shop.

8. Two key stations are located on or near double fire exit doors. One of them is key station No. 12.
   The *other* is key station No.

   A. 13   B. 14   C. 17   D. 18

9. If a security officer took a drink of water, he would *MOST* likely do so at a location closest to key station No.

   A. 12   B. 14   C. 16   D. 17

10. A delivery of $759.00 worth of supplies would *MOST* likely be made to a location which is closest to key station No.

    A. 13   B. 14   C. 16   D. 18

11. A fire exit door will *NOT* be found at key station No.

    A. 12   B. 13   C. 15   D. 17

12. When preparing a report, a security officer should generally make *at least* one extra copy so that

    A. it can be sent to a newspaper
    B. there will be no mistakes made
    C. a personal record can be kept
    D. the information in the report can be discussed by all other security officers

13. In writing a report about a storeroom robbery by several men, the LEAST important of the following information is

   A. the number of men involved
   B. a list of the items that were stolen
   C. how the men entered the storeroom
   D. how many lights were left on by the robbers

Questions 14-19.

DIRECTIONS: Questions 14 to 19 are based on the paragraph REGISTRY SHEETS shown below. When answering these questions, refer to this paragraph.

REGISTRY SHEETS

Where registry sheets are in effect, the security officer must legibly print Authority employee's pass number, title, license and vehicle number, destination, time in and time out; and each Authority employee must sign his or her name. The same procedure is to be applied to visitors, except in place of a pass number each visitor will indicate his address or firm name; and visitors must also sign waivers. Information is to be obtained from driver's license, firm credential card, or any other appropriate identification, All visitors must state their purpose for entering upon the property. If they desire to visit anyone, verification must be made before entry is permitted. All persons signing sheet must sign in when entering upon the property, and sign out again when leaving. The security officer will, at the end of his tour, draw a horizontal line across the entire sheet after his last entry, indicating the end of one tour and the beginning of another. At the top of each sheet the security officer will enter the number of entries made during his tour, the sheet number, post, and date. Sheets are to begin with number 1 on the first day of the month, and should be kept in numerical order. Each security officer will read the orders at each post to see whether any changes are made and at which hours control sheets are in effect.

14. Waivers need NOT be signed by

   A. Authority employees   B. vendors
   C. reporters   D. salesmen

15. All visitors are required to state

   A. whether they have a criminal record
   B. the reason for their visit
   C. the reason they are not bonded
   D. whether they have ever worked for the Authority

16. In the paragraph, the statement is made that "verification must be made before entry is permitted." The word verification means, most nearly,

   A. allowance   B. confirmation   C. refusal   D. disposal

17. A security officer must draw a horizontal line across the entire registry sheet in order to show that

   A. he is being replaced to check a disturbance outside
   B. the last tour for the day has been completed
   C. one tour is ending and another is beginning
   D. a visitor has finished his business and is leaving

18. At the top of a registry sheet, it is NOT necessary for a security officer to list the

    A. tour number
    B. number of entries made
    C. sheet number
    D. date

19. A security officer should check at which hours control sheets are in effect by reading

    A. registry sheet number 1, on the first day of each month
    B. the orders at each post
    C. the time in and time out that each person has entered on the registry sheet
    D. the last entry made on the registry sheet used before the start of his tour

20. Assume that after working as a security officer for some time, your foreman is replaced by a new foreman.
    If this new foreman insists on explaining to you the procedure for doing a job which you know how to do very well, you should listen to the new foreman MAINLY because

    A. you may catch him in an error and thus prove you know your job
    B. it is wise to humor a foreman even when he is wrong
    C. you can do the job the way you like after the foreman leaves
    D. it will be your responsibility to perform the job the way the new foreman wants it done

21. All security officers are instructed that whenever they report an accident to the main office by telephone, prior to preparing their written accident report, they should request the name of the person receiving the call and also make a note of the time.
    The MAIN purpose of this precaution is to fix responsibility for the

    A. cause of the accident
    B. recording of the accident at the main office
    C. accuracy of the accident report
    D. preparation of the written report

22. One of your duties as a security officer will be to compile the facts about an accident in a written report. The LEAST important item to include in such an accident report is

    A. the people involved
    B. what action you took
    C. the extent of personal injuries
    D. why you think the accident happened

23. It is MOST important for a written report to be

    A. accurate
    B. brief
    C. detailed
    D. properly punctuated

24. In a large bus shop where many security officers are used, each security officer is required to do his work in a definite prescribed manner MAINLY because

    A. this practice insures discipline
    B. no other method will work
    C. this practice will keep the security officer from being inattentive on the job
    D. there will be less need for the security officers to consult with their supervisors

25. When an unusual situation arises on the job, and it would take too long for you to contact your foreman for advice, the BEST procedure for you to follow is to

   A. play it safe and take no action
   B. confer with another security officer
   C. check your rule book for the proper procedure
   D. act according to your best judgment

26. At the scene of an accident it is good first-aid procedure to treat the most badly injured person first. Of the following injured people, the person LEAST in need of immediate care is one who

   A. is bleeding rapidly
   B. finds great difficulty in breathing
   C. appears to have sprained an ankle
   D. complains of severe pains in his chest

Questions 27-32.

DIRECTIONS: Questions 27 to 32 are based on the paragraph THEFT shown below. When answering these questions, refer to this paragraph.

THEFT

A security officer must be alert at all times to discourage the willful removal of property and material of the Authority by individuals for self gain. Should a security officer detect such an individual, he should detain him and immediately call the supervisor at that location. No force should be used during the process of detainment. However, should the individual bolt from the premises, the security officer will be expected to offer some clues for his apprehension. Therefore, he should try to remember some characteristic traits about the individual, such as clothing, height, coloring, speech, and how he made his approach. Unusual characteristics such as a scar or a limp are most important. If a car is used, the security officer should take the license plate number of said car. Above information should be supplied to the responding peace officer and the special inspection control desk. In desolate locations, the security officer should first call the police and then the special inspection control desk. Any security officer having information of the theft should contact the director of special inspection by telephone or by mail. This information will be kept confidential if desired.

27. A security officer is required to be attentive on the job at all times, MAINLY to

   A. get as much work done as possible
   B. prevent the stealing of Authority property
   C. show his supervisor that he is doing a good job
   D. prevent any other security officer from patrolling the area to which he is assigned

28. In the second sentence, the word detain means, most nearly,

   A. delay   B. avoid   C. call   D. report

29. The prescribed course of action a security officer should take when he discovers a person stealing Authority property is to

   A. make sure that all gates are closed to prevent the thief from escaping
   B. detain the thief and quickly call the supervisor

C. use his club to keep the thief there until the police arrive
D. call another security officer for assistance

30. The MOST useful of the following descriptions of a runaway thief would be that he is a

    A. tall man who runs fast
    B. man with blue eyes
    C. man with black hair
    D. tall man who limps

31. The license plate number of a car which is used by a thief to escape should be reported by & security officer to the responding peace officer *and* the

    A. director of protection agents
    B. security officer's supervisor
    C. special inspection control desk
    D. department of motor vehicles

32. A security officer patrolling a desolate area has spotted a thief. The security officer should FIRST call

    A. his supervisor
    B. the police
    C. the special inspection control desk
    D. the director of special inspection

33. It is very important that Authority officials be given legible hand-written reports on unusual occurrences if there is no time to type them up.
    According to the above statement about hand-written reports, it would be MOST useful if a security officer, when writing a report,

    A. did not write on the back of the page
    B. did not use big words
    C. wrote concisely
    D. wrote out all the information clearly

34. A security officer sees a youth marking up the wall surrounding Authority property. He should FIRST

    A. tell the youth to stop
    B. arrest the youth
    C. call a policeman
    D. punish the youth

35. If an alarm goes off and a security officer observes a van speeding away from a storeroom, the information that would be LEAST helpful in identifying the van would be the

    A. color of the van
    B. approximate speed at which the van passed his post
    C. state and the license plate number of the van
    D. manufacturer and model of the van

36. A security officer notices that a power line, knocked down by a storm, has electrified a steel flagpole. After notifying his supervisor, of the following it would be BEST to

    A. put a wooden "caution" sign on the flagpole and call the Fire Department
    B. remove the wire from the flagpole
    C. stay near the flagpole and warn everyone not to go near the flagpole
    D. say nothing about it until his supervisor arrives

37. Another Authority employee informs a security officer, who is on duty at the entrance to an Authority bus depot, that he has found a bomb in the locker room. The security officer should FIRST

    A. investigate to see if it is actually a bomb
    B. clear the area of persons in or near the locker room
    C. question the man closely to determine if he really saw a bomb
    D. call the Bomb Squad for instructions on handling bombs

37.____

38. In MOST cases, a written report on an accident is *better* than an oral report because a written report

    A. can be referred to later
    B. takes less time to prepare
    C. includes more of the facts
    D. reduces the number of court cases

38.____

39. A report of an accident is MOST likely to be accurate if written by the security officer

    A. long after the event
    B. after taking about a week to make sure he has all the facts
    C. immediately after the event
    D. after thoroughly discussing the event with others for several days

39.____

40. The gross weight of a carton and its contents is 830.2 pounds. If the weight of the carton alone is 98.7 pounds, the net weight of the contents of the carton is

    A. 731.5 pounds   B. 732.5 pounds
    C. 741.5 pounds   D. 831.5 pounds

40.____

KEY (CORRECT ANSWERS)

1. C	11. C	21. B	31. C
2. C	12. C	22. D	32. B
3. D	13. D	23. A	33. D
4. C	14. A	24. D	34. A
5. B	15. B	25. D	35. B
6. A	16. B	26. C	36. C
7. D	17. C	27. B	37. B
8. C	18. A	28. A	38. A
9. B	19. B	29. B	39. C
10. C	20. D	30. D	40. A

TEST 2

DIRECTIONS: Each question or incomplete statement is followed by several suggested answers or completions. Select the one that *BEST* answers the question or completes the statement. *PRINT THE LETTER OF THE CORRECT ANSWER TN THE SPACE AT THE RIGHT.*

Questions 1-10.

DIRECTIONS: Read the DESCRIPTION OF ACCIDENT carefully. Then answer Questions 1 to 10, inclusive, using only this information in picking your answer.

DESCRIPTION OF ACCIDENT

On Friday, May 9th, at about 2:30 p.m, Bus Operator Joe Able, badge no, 1234, was operating his half-filled bus, Authority no. 5678, northbound along Fifth Ave., when a green Ford truck, N.Y. license no. 9012, driven by Sam Wood, came out of an Authority storeroom entrance into the path of the bus. To avoid hitting the truck, Joe Able turned his steering wheel sharply to the left, causing his bus to cross the solid white line into the opposite lane where the bus crashed head-on into a black 1975 Mercury, N.Y. license no. 3456, driven by Bill Green. The crash caused the Mercury to sideswipe a blue VW, N.J. license 7890, driven by Jim White, which was double-parked while he made a delivery. The sudden movement of the bus caused one of the passengers, Mrs. Jane Smith, to fall, striking her head on one of the seats, Joe Able blew his horn vigorously to summon aid and Security Officer Fred Norton, badge no. 9876, and Stockman Al Blue, badge no. 5432, came out of the storeroom and rendered assistance. While Norton gave Mrs. Smith first aid, Blue summoned an ambulance for Green. A tow truck removed Green's car and Able found that the bus could operate under its own power, so he returned to the garage.

1. The Ford truck was driven by
   A. Able   B. Green   C. Wood   D. White

2. The Authority no. of the bus was
   A. 1234   B. 5678   C. 9012   D. 3456

3. The bus was driven by
   A. Able   B. Green   C. Wood   D. White

4. The license no. of the VW was
   A. 9012   B. 3456   C. 7890   D. 5432

5. The horn of the bus summoned
   A. Blue   B. Green   C. White   D. Smith

6. The badge no. of the security officer was
   A. 5432   B. 5678   C. 1234   D. 9876

7. The Mercury was driven by
   A. Smith   B. Norton   C. White   D. Green

8. The bus was traveling

   A. North   B. East   C. South   D. West

9. The vehicle towed away was a

   A. bus   B. Ford   C. Mercury   D. VW

10. Mrs. Smith hurt her

    A. head   B. back   C. arm   D. leg

11. If more than one security officer is involved in an incident, each is required to write a report giving his version of what happened. By having *both* reports submitted, the information gathered

    A. should be more complete
    B. should clear the Authority from any blame
    C. cannot be disputed
    D. will not be opinionated

12. If a security officer gets $5.42 per hour, and $8.13 per hour for overtime work, his *gross* salary for a week in which he works 5 hours over his regular 40 hours is

    A. $216.80   B. $243.90   C. $257.45   D. $325.20

13. It takes 2 min. 45 sec. for a security officer to travel to his first clock station, 3 min. to get to the second, 2 min. to get to the third, 5 1/2 min. to get to the fourth, and 4 min. 15 sec. to get from the fourth back to the starting point.
    Neglecting the time spent at each clock station, the *TOTAL* time needed to make one round tour is

    A. 16 min. 45 sec.   B. 17 min. 15 sec.
    C. 17 min. 30 sec.   D. 18 min.

Questions 14-20.

DIRECTIONS: Questions 14 to 20 are based on the rules listed below and are numbered 1 to 7. Each question gives a situation in which a security officer has disobeyed at least one rule. For each question, select from among the four choices the number of a rule which the security officer has disobeyed.

Rule Number 1: A security officer is subject to the orders of foremen (security officer) and of employees assigned to the special inspection control desk.

Rule Number 2: A security officer must protect system properties against fire, theft, vandalism, and unauthorized entrance.

Rule Number 3: A security officer is responsible for all equipment and other property entrusted to him and must see that such equipment is kept in good condition.

Rule Number 4: A security officer must give information about an accident only to authorized Authority officials.

Rule Number 5: A security officer must be attired in the prescribed uniform with badge displayed at all times while on duty.

Rule Number 6: A security officer must remain on duty during his entire tour and must therefore eat lunch on the job.

Rule Number 7: A security officer must not allow another employee to perform any part of his duties without proper authority.

14. While investigating a noise in the parking lot at night, Security Officer Johnson could not see very well because his flashlight was not in working order. Johnson disobeyed Rule Number

    A. 1 B. 3 C. 5 D. 7

15. Without getting permission to do so, Security Officer Simpson went to the locker room to get his lunch and let the porter, Baxter, check the credentials of a truck driver whose truck was about to enter Authority property. Simpson disobeyed Rule Number

    A. 1 B. 3 C. 5 D. 7

16. After being told by his foreman to check the door of Storeroom No. 15 before leaving, Security Officer Roscoe went off duty before seeing whether or not the door was properly locked. Roscoe disobeyed Rule Number

    A. 1 B. 4 C. 6 D. 7

17. Security Officer Andrews removed his badge ten minutes before going off duty. Andrews disobeyed Rule Number

    A. 2 B. 4 C. 5 D. 6

18. Security Officer Paul left his post inside the train yard in order to make a personal telephone call. As a result, Paul disobeyed Rule Number

    A. 2 B. 4 C. 5 D. 7

19. Security Officer Burroughs gave a newspaper reporter details of an accident that occurred on his post. Burroughs disobeyed Rule Number

    A. 1 B. 2 C. 3 D. 4

20. Security Officer Grenich left his post unattended and went across the street to a diner, since he left his lunch at home. Grenich disobeyed Rule Number

    A. 4 B. 5 C. 6 D. 7

Questions 21-25.

DIRECTIONS: Questions 21 to 25 are based on the UNUSUAL OCCURRENCE REPORT given below. Five phrases in the report have been removed and are listed below the report as 1. through 5. In each of the five places where phrases of the report have been left out, the number of a question has been inserted. For each question, select the number of the missing phrase which would make the report read correctly.

4 (#2)

UNUSUAL OCCURRENCE REPORT

Post 20A
Tour 12 a.m.-8 a.m.
Date August 13

Location of Occurrence: Storeroom #55

REMARKS: While making rounds this morning I thought that I heard some strange sounds coming from Storeroom #55. Upon investigation, I saw that 21 and that the door to the storeroom was slightly opened. At 2:45 a.m. I 22 .

Suddenly two men jumped out from 23 , dropped the tools which they were holding, and made a dash for the door. I ordered them to stop, but they just kept running.

I was able to get a good look at both of them. One man was wearing a green jacket and had a full beard and the other was short and had blond hair. Immediately, I called the police and about two minutes later I notified 24 . I 25 the police arrived and I gave them the complete details of the incident.

Security Officer Donald Rimson 23807
Signature Pass No.

1. the special inspection control desk
2. behind some crates
3. the lock had been tampered with
4. remained at the storeroom until
5. entered the storeroom and began to look around

21. A. 1   B. 3   C. 4   D. 5   21.____

22. A. 2   B. 3   C. 4   D. 5   22.____

23. A. 1   B. 2   C. 3   D. 4   23.____

24. A. 1   B. 2   C. 3   D. 4   24.____

25. A. 2   B. 3   C. 4   D. 5   25.____

26. Employees using supplies from a first-aid kit are generally required to submit an immediate report on what happened and what supplies were used.
Of the following, the MOST important reason for this regulation is to   26.____

   A. make sure that supplies which are used are replaced
   B. prevent theft
   C. see that the correct employee gets credit for taking action
   D. identify the person who last used the kit

27. The log book of a security officer stationed at an entry gate shows 47 entries in two hours. At this rate, the number of entries in eight hours is   27.____

   A. 108   B. 168   C. 188   D. 376

28. A truck driver leaving Authority property has a requisition form showing 14 cartons of pencils, 12 cartons of pens, 27 cartons of envelopes, and 39 cartons of writing pads. If an actual count of the cartons on the truck shows only 77 cartons, the number of cartons missing is   28.____

   A. 15   B. 14   C. 12   D. 5

29. It is NOT advisable to move an injured man before the arrival of a doctor if the man has

   A. a severe nosebleed
   B. burns over 3% of his body
   C. fainted from the heat
   D. possibly injured his spine

30. While making rounds during daylight hours, a security officer notices that one of the floodlights in the parking lot has been left on. The security officer should

   A. turn the light off because it will cost him his job if his foreman finds out about this
   B. turn the light off, because it is not needed
   C. leave the light on and call his foreman to investigate
   D. leave the light on to make it easier for him to see anything which looks suspicious

31. A security officer comes upon an empty fire extinguisher while making his rounds. Of the following, it is MOST important that he

   A. ignore it, since mentioning this might get someone into trouble
   B. make a note not to use that extinguisher in case of a fire
   C. report it to the next security officer who relieves him
   D. report it to his foreman

32. The windows of the booth used by a security officer must be kept clean and clear of any obstructions at all times. The MOST obvious reason for this is to

   A. enable anyone passing by the booth to look into it and see who is on duty
   B. allow as much daylight as possible to enter the booth so that a security officer can conserve electricity by keeping booth lights turned off
   C. enable a security officer to see what is happening outside of the booth
   D. make certain that a security officer makes a good impression on inspectors who are passing by the booth

33. A security officer must be completely familiar with door schedules (when the door must be locked and when open), particularly during hours when employees are reporting for work.
   If a security officer does not know all door schedules for his post it would be BEST for him to

   A. quickly get a copy of the door schedule from the security officer who will relieve him
   B. check the bulletin board at a nearby post to see if he can get a copy of the door schedules
   C. let his foreman know about it immediately, so the foreman can give him the information he needs
   D. check the rules and regulations book for the information

Questions 34-37.

DIRECTIONS: Questions 34 to 37 inclusive are based on the paragraph FIRE FIGHTING shown below. When answering these questions, refer to this paragraph.

FIRE FIGHTING

A security officer should remember the cardinal rule that water or soda acid fire extinguishers should not be used on any electrical fire, and apply it in the case of a fire near the third rail. In addition, security officers should familiarize themselves with all available fire alarms and fire-fighting equipment within their assigned posts. Use of the fire alarm should bring responding Fire Department apparatus quickly to the scene. Familiarity with the fire-fighting equipment near his post would help in putting out incipient fires. Any man calling for the Fire Department should remain outside so that he can direct the Fire Department to the fire. As soon as possible thereafter, the special inspection desk must be notified and a complete written report of the fire, no matter how small, must be submitted to this office. The security officer must give the exact time and place it started, who discovered it, how it was extinguished, the damage done, cause of same, list of any injured persons with the extent of their injuries, and the name of the Fire Chief in charge. All defects noticed by the security officer concerning the fire alarm or any firefighting equipment must be reported to the special inspection department.

34. It would be proper to use water to put out a fire in a(n)

    A. electric motor
    B. electric switch box
    C. waste paper trash can
    D. electric generator

35. After calling the Fire Department from a street box to report a fire, the security officer should then

    A. return to the fire and help put it out
    B. stay outside and direct the Fire Department to the fire
    C. find a phone and call his boss
    D. write out a report for the special inspection desk

36. A security officer is required to submit a complete written report of a fire

    A. two weeks after the fire
    B. the day following the fire
    C. as soon as possible
    D. at his convenience

37. In his report of a fire, it is NOT necessary for the security officer to state

    A. time and place of the fire
    B. who discovered the fire
    C. the names of persons injured
    D. quantity of Fire Department equipment used

38. While making afternoon rounds, a security officer climbs a stairway which has a loose banister.
    To avoid having someone injured, the security officer should

    A. inform his foreman of the hazard so that it can be corrected
    B. fix the banister himself, since it can probably be fixed quickly
    C. block the stairway with rope at the top and bottom so that no one else can use it
    D. put up a caution sign in the hallway leading to the stairway

39. If, while on duty, a security officer sees an accident which results in injuries to Authority employees, it would be most important for him to FIRST

   A. render all possible first-aid to the injured
   B. record the exact time the accident happened
   C. write out an accident report
   D. try to find out what caused the accident

40. If a security officer has many accidents, no matter what shift or location he is assigned to, the MOST likely reason for this is

   A. lack of safety devices
   B. not enough safety posters
   C. inferior equipment and materials
   D. careless work practices

KEY (CORRECT ANSWERS)

1.	C	11.	A	21.	B	31.	D
2.	B	12.	C	22.	D	32.	C
3.	A	13.	C	23.	B	33.	C
4.	C	14.	B	24.	A	34.	C
5.	A	15.	D	25.	C	35.	B
6.	D	16.	A	26.	A	36.	C
7.	D	17.	C	27.	C	37.	D
8.	A	18.	A	28.	A	38.	A
9.	C	19.	D	29.	D	39.	A
10.	A	20.	C	30.	B	40.	D

EXAMINATION SECTION
TEST 1

DIRECTIONS: Each question or incomplete statement is followed by several suggested answers or completions. Select the one that BEST answers the question or completes the statement. *PRINT THE LETTER OF THE CORRECT ANSWER IN THE SPACE AT THE RIGHT.*

1. The officer who investigates accidents is always required to make a complete and accurate report.
   Of the following, the BEST reason for this procedure is to

   A. protect the operating agency against possible false claims
   B. provide a file of incidents which can be used as basic material for an accident prevention campaign
   C. provide the management with concrete evidence of violations of the rules by employees
   D. indicate what repairs need to be made

   1.____

2. It is suggested that an officer keep all persons away from the area of an accident until an investigation has been completed.
   This suggested procedure is

   A. *good;* witnesses will be more likely to agree on a single story
   B. *bad;* such action blocks traffic flow and causes congestion
   C. *good;* objects of possible use as evidence will be protected from damage or loss
   D. *bad;* the flow of normal pedestrian traffic provides an opportunity for an investigator to determine the cause of the accident

   2.____

3. A man having business with your agency is arguing with you and accuses you of being prejudiced against him. Although you explain to him that this is not so, he demands to see your supervisor.
   Of the following, the BEST course of action for you to take is to

   A. continue arguing with him until you have worn him out or convinced him
   B. take him to your supervisor
   C. ignore him and walk away from him to another part of the office
   D. escort him out of the office

   3.____

4. An officer receives instructions from his supervisor which he does not fully understand.
   For the officer to ask for a further explanation would be

   A. *good;* chiefly because his supervisor will be impressed with his interest in his work
   B. *poor;* chiefly because the time of the supervisor will be needlessly wasted
   C. *good;* chiefly because proper performance depends on full understanding of the work to be done
   D. *poor;* chiefly because officers should be able to think for themselves

   4.____

5. A person is making a complaint to an officer which seems unreasonable and of little importance.
   Of the following, the BEST action for the officer to take is to

   5.____

A. criticize the person making the complaint for taking up his valuable time
B. laugh over the matter to show that the complaint is minor and silly
C. tell the person that anyone responsible for his grievance will be prosecuted
D. listen to the person making the complaint and tell him that the matter will be investigated

6. A member of the department shall not indulge in intoxicating liquor while in uniform. A member of the department is not required to wear a uniform, and a uniformed member while out of uniform shall not indulge in intoxicants to an extent unfitting him for duty.
Of the following, the MOST correct interpretation of this rule is that a

   A. member, off duty, not in uniform, may drink intoxicating liquor
   B. member, not on duty, but in uniform, may drink intoxicating liquor
   C. member, on duty, in uniform, may drink intoxicants
   D. uniformed member, in civilian clothes, may not drink intoxicants

6.____

7. You have a suggestion for an important change which you believe will improve a certain procedure in your agency. Of the following, the next course of action for you to take is to

   A. try it out yourself
   B. submit the suggestion to your immediate supervisor
   C. write a letter to the head of your agency asking for his approval
   D. wait until you are asked for suggestions before submitting this one

7.____

8. An officer shall study maps and literature concerning his assigned area and the streets and points of interest nearby.
Of the following, the BEST reason for this rule is that

   A. the officer will be better able to give correct information to persons desiring it
   B. the officer will be better able to drive a vehicle in the area
   C. the officer will not lose interest in his work
   D. supervisors will not need to train the officers in this subject

8.____

9. In asking a witness to a crime to identify a suspect, it is a common practice to place the suspect with a group of persons and ask the witness to pick out the person in question.
Of the following, the BEST reason for this practice is that it will

   A. make the identification more reliable than if the witness were shown the suspect alone
   B. protect the witness against reprisals
   C. make sure that the witness is telling the truth
   D. help select other participants in the crime at the same time

9.____

10. It is most important for all officers to obey the "Rules and Regulations" of their agency.
Of the following, the BEST reason for this statement is that

    A. supervisors will not need to train their new officers
    B. officers will never have to use their own judgment
    C. uniform procedures will be followed
    D. officers will not need to ask their supervisors for assistance

10.____

Questions 11-13.

DIRECTIONS: Answer questions 11 to 13 SOLELY on the basis of the following paragraph.

All members of the police force must recognize that the people, through their representatives, hire and pay the police and that, as in any other employment, there must exist a proper employer-employee relationship. The police officer must understand that the essence of a correct police attitude is a willingness to serve, but at the same time, he should distinguish between service and servility, and between courtesy and softness. He must be firm but also courteous, avoiding even an appearance of rudeness. He should develop a position that is friendly and unbiased, pleasant and sympathetic, in his relations with the general public, but firm and impersonal on occasions calling for regulation and control. A police officer should understand that his primary purpose is to prevent violations, not to arrest people. He should recognize the line of demarcation between a police function and passing judgment which is a court function. On the other side, a public that cooperates with the police, that supports them in their efforts and that observes laws and regulations, may be said to have a desirable attitude.

11. In accordance with this paragraph, the PROPER attitude for a police officer to take is to   11.____

    A. be pleasant and sympathetic at all times
    B. be friendly, firm, and impartial
    C. be stern and severe in meting out justice to all
    D. avoid being rude, except in those cases where the public is uncooperative

12. Assume that an officer is assigned by his superior officer to a busy traffic intersection and   12.____
    is warned to be on the lookout for motorists who skip the light or who are speeding.
    According to this paragraph, it would be proper for the officer in this assignment to

    A. give a summons to every motorist whose ear was crossing when the light changed
    B. hide behind a truck and wait for drivers who violate traffic laws
    C. select at random motorists who seem to be impatient and lecture them sternly on traffic safety
    D. stand on post in order to deter violations and give offenders a summons or a warning as required

13. According to this paragraph, a police officer must realize that the primary purpose of   13.____
    police work is to

    A. provide proper police service in a courteous manner
    B. decide whether those who violate the law should be punished
    C. arrest those who violate laws
    D. establish a proper employer-employee relationship

Questions 14-15.

DIRECTIONS: Answer questions 14 and 15 SOLELY on the basis of the following paragraph.

If a motor vehicle fails to pass inspection, the owner will be given a rejection notice by the inspection station. Repairs must be made within ten days after this notice is issued. It is not necessary to have the required adjustment or repairs made at the station where the inspection occurred. The vehicle may be taken to any other garage. Re-inspection after repairs may be made at any official inspection station, not necessarily the same station which made the initial inspection. The registration of any motor vehicle for which an inspection sticker has not been obtained as required, or which is not repaired and inspected within ten days after inspection indicates defects, is subject to suspension. A vehicle cannot be used on public highways while its registration is under suspension.

14. According to the above paragraph, the owner of a car which does NOT pass inspection must

   A. have repairs made at the same station which rejected his car
   B. take the car to another station and have it re-inspected
   C. have repairs made anywhere and then have the car re-inspected
   D. not use the car on a public highway until the necessary repairs have been made

15. According to the above paragraph, the one of the following which may be cause for suspension of the registration of a vehicle is that

   A. an inspection sticker was issued before the rejection notice had been in force for ten days
   B. it was not re-inspected by the station that rejected it originally
   C. it was not re-inspected either by the station that rejected it originally or by the garage which made the repairs
   D. it has not had defective parts repaired within ten days after inspection

Questions 16-20.

DIRECTIONS: Answer questions 16 to 20 SOLELY on the basis of the following paragraph.

If we are to study crime in its widest social setting, we will find a variety of conduct which, although criminal in the legal sense, is not offensive to the moral conscience of a considerable number of persons. Traffic violations, for example, do not brand the offender as guilty of moral offense. In fact, the recipient of a traffic ticket is usually simply the subject of some good-natured joking by his friends. Although there may be indignation among certain groups of citizens against gambling and liquor law violations, these activities are often tolerated, if not openly supported, by the more numerous residents of the community. Indeed, certain social and service clubs regularly conduct gambling games and lotteries for the purpose of raising funds. Some communities regard violations involving the sale of liquor with little concern in order to profit from increased license fees and taxes paid by dealers. The thousand and one forms of political graft and corruption which infest our urban centers only occasionally arouse public condemnation and official action.

16. According to the paragraph, all types of illegal conduct are

   A. condemned by all elements of the community
   B. considered a moral offense, although some are tolerated by a few citizens
   C. violations of the law, but some are acceptable to certain elements of the community
   D. found in a social setting which is not punishable by law

17. According to the paragraph, traffic violations are generally considered by society as

   A. crimes requiring the maximum penalty set by the law
   B. more serious than violations of the liquor laws

C. offenses against the morals of the community
D. relatively minor offenses requiring minimum punishment

18. According to the paragraph, a lottery conducted for the purpose of raising funds for a church

    A. is considered a serious violation of law
    B. may be tolerated by a community which has laws against gambling
    C. may be conducted under special laws demanded by the more numerous residents of a community
    D. arouses indignation in most communities

19. On the basis of the paragraph, the MOST likely reaction in the community to a police raid on a gambling casino would be

    A. more an attitude of indifference than interest in the raid
    B. general approval of the raid
    C. condemnation of the raid by most people
    D. demand for further action since this raid is not sufficient to end gambling activities

20. The one of the following which BEST describes the central thought of this paragraph and would be MOST suitable as a title for it is

    A. CRIME AND THE POLICE
    B. PUBLIC CONDEMNATION OF GRAFT AND CORRUPTION
    C. GAMBLING IS NOT ALWAYS A VICIOUS BUSINESS
    D. PUBLIC ATTITUDE TOWARD LAW VIOLATIONS

Questions 21-23.

DIRECTIONS: Answer questions 21 to 23 SOLELY on the basis of the following paragraph.

The law enforcement agency is one of the most important agencies in the field of juvenile delinquency prevention. This is so not because of the social work connected with this problem, however, for this is not a police matter, but because the officers are usually the first to come in contact with the delinquent. The manner of arrest and detention makes a deep impression upon him and affects his life-long attitude toward society and the law. The juvenile court is perhaps the most important agency in this work. Contrary to the general opinion, however, it is not primarily concerned with putting children into correctional schools. The main purpose of the juvenile court is to save the child and to develop his emotional make-up in order that he can grow up to be a decent and well-balanced citizen. The system of probation is the means whereby the court seeks to accomplish these goals.

21. According to this paragraph, police work is an important part of a program to prevent juvenile delinquency because

    A. social work is no longer considered important in juvenile delinquency prevention
    B. police officers are the first to have contact with the delinquent
    C. police officers jail the offender in order to be able to change his attitude toward society and the law
    D. it is the first step in placing the delinquent in jail

22. According to this paragraph, the CHIEF purpose of the juvenile court is to   22.____

    A. punish the child for his offense
    B. select a suitable correctional school for the delinquent
    C. use available means to help the delinquent become a better person
    D. provide psychiatric care for the delinquent

23. According to this paragraph, the juvenile court directs the development of delinquents   23.____
    under its care CHIEFLY by

    A. placing the child under probation
    B. sending the child to a correctional school
    C. keeping the delinquent in prison
    D. returning the child to his home

Questions 24-27.

DIRECTIONS: Answer questions 24 to 27 SOLELY on the basis of the following paragraph.

When a vehicle has been disabled in the tunnel, the officer on patrol in this zone shall press the EMERGENCY TRUCK light button. In the fast lane, red lights will go on throughout the tunnel; in the slow lane, amber lights will go on throughout the tunnel. The yellow zone light will go on at each signal control station throughout the tunnel and will flash the number of the zone in which the stoppage has occurred. A red flashing pilot light will appear only at the signal control station at which the EMERGENCY TRUCK button was pressed. The emergency garage will receive an audible and visual signal indicating the signal control station at which the EMERGENCY TRUCK button was pressed. The garage officer shall acknowledge receipt of the signal by pressing the acknowledgment button. This will cause the pilot light at the operated signal control station in the tunnel to cease flashing and to remain steady. It is an answer to the officer at the operated signal control station that the emergency truck is responding to the call.

24. According to this paragraph, when the EMERGENCY TRUCK light button is pressed,   24.____

    A. amber lights will go on in every lane throughout the tunnel
    B. emergency signal lights will go on only in the lane in which the disabled vehicle happens to be
    C. red lights will go on in the fast lane throughout the tunnel
    D. pilot lights at all signal control stations will turn amber

25. According to this paragraph, the number of the zone in which the stoppage has occurred   25.____
    is flashed

    A. immediately after all the lights in the tunnel turn red
    B. by the yellow zone light at each signal control station
    C. by the emergency truck at the point of stoppage
    D. by the emergency garage

26. According to this paragraph, an officer near the disabled vehicle will know that the emer-   26.____
    gency tow truck is coming when

    A. the pilot light at the operated signal control station appears and flashes red
    B. an audible signal is heard in the tunnel

C. the zone light at the operated signal control station turns red
D. the pilot light at the operated signal control station becomes steady

27. Under the system described in the paragraph, it would be CORRECT to come to the conclusion that   27._____

   A. officers at all signal control stations are expected to acknowledge that they have received the stoppage signal
   B. officers at all signal control stations will know where the stoppage has occurred
   C. all traffic in both lanes of that side of the tunnel in which the stoppage has occurred must stop until the emergency truck has arrived
   D. there are two emergency garages, each able to respond to stoppages in traffic going in one particular direction

Questions 28-30.

DIRECTIONS: Answer questions 28 to 30 SOLELY on the basis of the following paragraphs.

In cases of accident, it is most important for an officer to obtain the name, age, residence, occupation, and a full description of the person injured, names and addresses of witnesses. He shall also obtain a statement of the attendant circumstances. He shall carefully note contributory conditions, if any, such as broken pavement, excavation, tights not burning, snow and ice on the roadway, etc. He shall enter all facts in his memorandum book and on Form 17 or Form 18 and promptly transmit the original of the form to his superior officer and the duplicate to headquarters.

An officer shall render reasonable assistance to sick or injured persons. If the circumstances appear to require the services of a physician, he shall summon a physician by telephoning the superior officer on duty and notifying him of the apparent nature of the illness or accident and the location where the physician will be required. He may summon other officers to assist if circumstances warrant.

In case of an accident or where a person is sick on city property, an officer shall obtain the information necessary to fill out card Form 18 and record this in his memorandum book and promptly telephone the facts to his superior officer. He shall deliver the original card at the expiration of his tour to his superior officer and transmit the duplicate to headquarters.

28. According to this quotation, the MOST important consideration in any report on a case of accident or injury is to   28._____

   A. obtain all the facts
   B. telephone his superior officer at once
   C. obtain a statement of the attendant circumstances
   D. determine ownership of the property on which the accident occurred

29. According to this quotation, in the case of an accident on city property, the officer should always   29._____

   A. summon a physician before filling out any forms or making any entries in his memorandum book
   B. give his superior officer on duty a prompt report by telephone

C. immediately bring the original of Form 18 to his superior officer on duty
D. call at least one other officer to the scene to witness conditions

30. If the procedures stated in this quotation were followed for all accidents in the city, an impartial survey of accidents occurring during any period of time in this city may be MOST easily made by

   A. asking a typical officer to show you his memorandum book
   B. having a superior officer investigate whether contributory conditions mentioned by witnesses actually exist
   C. checking all the records of all superior officers
   D. checking the duplicate card files at headquarters

Questions 31-55.

DIRECTIONS: In each of questions 31 to 55, select the lettered word or phrase which means MOST NEARLY the same as the first word in the row.

31. RENDEZVOUS
   A. parade   B. neighborhood
   C. meeting place D. wander about

32. EMINENT
   A. noted   B. rich   C. rounded   D. nearby

33. CAUSTIC
   A. cheap   B. sweet   C. evil   D. sharp

34. BARTER
   A. annoy   B. trade   C. argue   D. cheat

35. APTITUDE
   A. friendliness   B. talent
   C. conceit   D. generosity

36. PROTRUDE
   A. project   B. defend   C. choke   D. boast

37. FORTITUDE
   A. disposition   B. restlessness
   C. courage   D. poverty

38. PRELUDE
   A. introduction   B. meaning
   C. prayer   D. secret

39. SECLUSION
   A. primitive   B. influence
   C. imagination   D. privacy

40. RECTIFY
    A. correct   B. construct   C. divide   D. scold
41. TRAVERSE
    A. rotate   B. compose   C. train   D. cross
42. ALLEGE
    A. raise   B. convict   C. declare   D. chase
43. MENIAL
    A. pleasant   B. unselfish
    C. humble   D. stupid
44. DEPLETE
    A. exhaust   B. gather   C. repay   D. close
45. ERADICATE
    A. construct   B. advise   C. destroy   D. exclaim
46. CAPITULATE
    A. cover   B. surrender   C. receive   D. execute
47. RESTRAIN
    A. restore   B. drive   C. review   D. limit
48. AMALGAMATE
    A. join   B. force   C. correct   D. clash
49. DEJECTED
    A. beaten   B. speechless
    C. weak   D. low-spirited
50. DETAIN
    A. hide   B. accuse   C. hold   D. mislead

KEY (CORRECT ANSWERS)

1. A	11. B	21. B	31. C	41. D
2. C	12. D	22. C	32. A	42. C
3. B	13. A	23. A	33. D	43. C
4. C	14. C	24. C	34. B	44. A
5. D	15. D	25. B	35. B	45. C
6. A	16. C	26. D	36. A	46. B
7. B	17. D	27. B	37. C	47. D
8. A	18. B	28. A	38. A	48. A
9. A	19. A	29. B	39. D	49. D
10. C	20. D	30. D	40. A	50. C

TEST 2

DIRECTIONS: Each question or incomplete statement is followed by several suggested answers or completions. Select the one that BEST answers the question or completes the statement. *PRINT THE LETTER OF THE CORRECT ANSWER IN THE SPACE AT THE RIGHT.*

1. AMPLE
    A. necessary   B. plentiful   C. protected   D. tasty

2. EXPEDITE
    A. sue   B. omit   C. hasten   D. verify

3. FRAGMENT
    A. simple tool   B. broken part
    C. basic outline   D. weakness

4. ADVERSARY
    A. thief   B. partner   C. loser   D. foe

5. ACHIEVE
    A. accomplish   B. begin   C. develop   D. urge

Questions 6-10.

DIRECTIONS: Answer Questions 6 to 10 on the basis of the information given in the table on the following page. The numbers which have been omitted from the table can be calculated from the other numbers which are given.

NUMBER OF DWELLING UNITS CONSTRUCTED

Year	Private one-family houses	In private apt. houses	In public housing	Total dwelling units
1996	4,500	500	600	5,600
1997	9,200	5,300	2,800	17,300
1998	8,900	12,800	6,800	28,500
1999	12,100	15,500	7,100	34,700
2000	?	12,200	14,100	39,200
2001	10,200	26,000	8,600	44,800
2002	10,300	17,900	7,400	35,600
2003	11,800	18,900	7,700	38,400
2004	12,700	22,100	8,400	43,200
2005	13,300	24,300	8,100	45,700
TOTALS	105,900	?	?	?

6. According to this table, the average number of public housing units constructed yearly during the period 1996 through 2005 was
    A. 7,160   B. 6,180   C. 7,610   D. 6,810

7. Of the following, the two years in which the number of private one-family homes constructed was GREATEST for the two years together is

   A. 1998 and 1999
   B. 1997 and 2003
   C. 1998 and 2004
   D. 2001 and 2002

8. For the entire period of 1996 through 2005, the total of all private one-family houses constructed exceeded the total of all public housing units constructed by

   A. 34,300   B. 45,700   C. 50,000   D. 83,900

9. Of the total number of private apartment house dwelling units constructed in the ten years given in the table, the percentage which was constructed in 2002 was MOST NEARLY

   A. 5%   B. 11%   C. 16%   D. 21%

10. Considering dwelling units of all types, the average number constructed annually in the period from 2001 through 2005 was GREATER than the average number constructed annually in the period from 1996 through 2000 by

    A. 16,480   B. 33,320   C. 79,300   D. 82,400

11. A car speeds through the toll entrance of a 2 1/4 mile long bridge without paying the toll and reaches the other end of the bridge 1 minute and 30 seconds later. The car was traveling MOST NEARLY at a rate of _____ miles per hour.

    A. 60   B. 70   C. 80   D. 90

12. During one week, 21,500 vehicles passed through the toll booths of a certain bridge. Of these, 550 were buses, 2,230 were trucks, and the rest were passenger cars. The toll charges were $3.50 for a passenger car, $7 for a truck and $14 for a bus. The total income for the week was

    A. $80,850   B. $88,830   C. $102,550   D. $109,550

13. A bullet fired from a revolver travels 100 feet the first second, and each succeeding second it travels a distance 10% less than during the immediately preceding second. The number of feet the bullet will have traveled at the end of the fourth second is MOST NEARLY

    A. 272   B. 320   C. 344   D. 360

14. An officer receives a uniform allowance of $500 a year in a lump sum. Of this amount, he spends $180 for a winter jacket and 40% of the remainder for two pairs of trousers. The officer now wishes to buy a winter overcoat which costs $240.
    The percentage of the purchase price of the overcoat by which he will be short is

    A. 20%   B. 25%   C. 48%   D. 60%

15. It has been suggested that small light cars can be used for certain kinds of police work. These light vehicles can run 30 miles per gallon of gasoline as contrasted with standard cars which run only 15 miles per gallon. Assume gasoline costs the city $3.75 per gallon. During 9,000 miles of travel, use of the small light car in preference to the standard car would result in a saving in gasoline costs of MOST NEARLY

    A. $1,125   B. $1,500   C. $1,875   D. $2,250

16. Out of a total of 34,750 felony complaints in 2006, 14,200 involved burglary. In 2005, there was a total of 32,300 felony complaints of which 12,800 were burglary. Of the increase in felonies from 2005 to 2006, the increase in burglaries comprised APPROXIMATELY

    A. 27%   B. 37%   C. 47%   D. 57%

    16.____

17. A certain city department has two offices which issue permits, one office handling twice as many applicants as the other. The smaller office grants permits to 40% of its applicants. The larger office handling twice as many applicants grants permits to 60% of its applicants.
    If there were 900 applicants at both offices together on a given day, the total number of permits granted by both offices would be MOST NEARLY

    A. 420   B. 450   C. 480   D. 510

    17.____

18. If a co-worker is not breathing after receiving an electric shock but is no longer in contact with the electricity, it is MOST important for you to

    A. avoid moving him
    B. wrap the victim in a blanket
    C. start artificial respiration promptly
    D. force him to take hot liquids

    18.____

19. Employees using supplies from one of the first-aid kits available throughout the building are required to submit an immediate report of the occurrence.
    Logical reasoning shows that the MOST important reason for this report is so that the

    A. supplies used will be sure to be replaced
    B. first-aid kit can be properly sealed again
    C. employee will be credited for his action
    D. record of first-aid supplies will be up-to-date

    19.____

20. The BEST IMMEDIATE first-aid treatment for a scraped knee is to

    A. apply plain vaseline   B. wash it with soap and water
    C. apply heat   D. use a knee splint

    20.____

21. Artificial respiration after a severe electrical shock is ALWAYS necessary when the shock results in

    A. unconsciousness   B. stoppage of breathing
    C. bleeding   D. a burn

    21.____

22. The authority gives some of its maintenance employees instruction in first aid.
    The MOST likely reason for doing this is to

    A. eliminate the need for calling a doctor in case of accident
    B. provide temporary emergency treatment in case of accident
    C. lower the cost of accidents to the authority
    D. reduce the number of accidents

    22.____

23. The BEST IMMEDIATE first aid if a chemical solution splashes into the eyes is to

    A. protect the eyes from the light by bandaging
    B. rub the eyes dry with a towel

    23.____

C. cause tears to flow by staring at a bright light
D. flush the eyes with large quantities of clean water

24. If you had to telephone for an ambulance because of an accident, the MOST important information for you to give the person who answered the telephone would be the

   A. exact time of the accident
   B. cause of the accident
   C. place where the ambulance is needed
   D. names and addresses of those injured

25. If a person has a deep puncture wound in his finger caused by a sharp nail, the BEST IMMEDIATE first aid procedure would be to

   A. encourage bleeding by exerting pressure around the injured area
   B. stop all bleeding
   C. prevent air from reaching the wound
   D. probe the wound for steel particles

26. In addition to cases of submersion, artificial respiration is a recommended first aid procedure for

   A. sunstroke   B. electrical shock   C. chemical poisoning   D. apoplexy

27. Assume that you are called on to render first aid to a man injured in an accident. You find he is bleeding profusely, is unconscious, and has a broken arm. There is a strong odor of alcohol about him.
    The FIRST thing for which you should treat him is the

   A. bleeding   B. unconsciousness   C. broken arm   D. alcoholism

28. In applying first aid for removal of a foreign body in the eye, an important precaution to be observed is NOT to

   A. attempt to wash out the foreign body
   B. bring the upper eyelid down over the lower
   C. rub the eye
   D. touch or attempt to remove a speck on the lower lid

29. The one of the following symptoms which is LEAST likely to indicate that a person involved in an accident requires first aid for shock is that

   A. he has fainted twice
   B. his face is red and flushed
   C. his skin is wet with sweat
   D. his pulse is rapid

30. When giving first aid to a person suffering from shock as a result of an auto accident, it is MOST important to

   A. massage him in order to aid blood circulation
   B. have him sip whiskey
   C. prop him up in a sitting position
   D. cover the person and keep him warm

Questions 31-34.

DIRECTIONS: Answer questions 31 to 34 SOLELY on the basis of the following paragraph.

Assume that you are an officer assigned to one large office which issues and receives applications for various permits and licenses. The office consists of one section where the necessary forms are issued; another section where fees are paid to a cashier; and desks where applicants are interviewed and their forms reviewed and completed. There is also a section containing tables and chairs where persons may sit and fill out their applications before being interviewed or paying the fees. your duties consist of answering simple questions, directing the public to the correct section of the office, and maintaining order.

31. A man who speaks English poorly asks you for assistance in obtaining and filling out an application for a permit. You should

    A. send him to an interviewer who can assist him
    B. try to determine what permit he wants and fill out the form for him
    C. refer the man to the office supervisor
    D. ask another applicant to help this person

31.____

32. The office becomes noisy and crowded, with people milling around waiting for service at the various sections.
    Of the following, the BEST action for you to take is to

    A. stand in a prominent place and in a loud voice request the people to be quiet
    B. direct all the people not being served to wait at the unoccupied tables until you call them
    C. line up the people in front of each section and keep the lines in good order
    D. tell the people to form a single line outside the office and let in a few at a time

32.____

33. A man who has just been denied a permit becomes angry and shouts that if he "knew the right people" he too could get a permit. His behavior is disturbing the office.
    Of the following, the BEST action for you to take is to

    A. order the man to leave at once since his business is done
    B. tell the man to be quiet and file another application
    C. suggest to the supervisor that a pamphlet be prepared explaining the requirements for permits in simple language
    D. ask an interviewer to explain the requirements for his permit to the person and his right of appeal

33.____

34. Just before the close of business, a man rushes in and insists on being interviewed for a permit because his present one expires that night.
    Of the following, the BEST action for you to take is to

    A. tell the man that the office is closed
    B. tell the man that there will be no penalty if he returns early the next morning
    C. inquire if an interviewer is still available to take care of him and send him to that desk
    D. tell the cashier to collect the fee and tell the man to return the next morning for an interview

34.____

35. Fingerprints are often taken of applicants for licenses. Of the following, the MOST valid reason for this procedure is that

    A. the license of someone who commits a crime can be more readily revoked
    B. applicants can be checked for possible criminal records
    C. it helps to make sure that the proper license fee is paid
    D. a complete employment record of the applicant is obtained

36. Assume that an officer is on patrol at 2 A.M. He notices that the night light inside one of the stores in a public building is out. The store is locked.
    Of the following, the FIRST action for him to take at this time is to

    A. continue on his patrol since the light probably burned out
    B. enter the store by any means possible so he can check it
    C. report the matter to his superior
    D. shine his flashlight through the window to look for anything unusual

37. In questioning a man suspected of having committed a theft, the BEST procedure for an officer to follow is to

    A. induce the man to express his feelings about the police, the courts, and his home environment
    B. threaten him with beatings when he refuses to answer your questions
    C. make any promises necessary to get him to confess
    D. remain calm and objective

38. As an officer, you are on duty in one of the offices of a large public building. A woman who has just finished her business with this office comes to you and reports that her son who was with her is missing.
    The one of the following which is the BEST action for you to take FIRST is to

    A. tell the mother that the child is probably all right and ask her to go to the local police station for help in finding the boy
    B. suggest that the mother wait in the office until the child turns up
    C. check nearby offices in an attempt to locate the child
    D. telephone the local police station and ask if any reports fitting the description of the child have been received

39. An officer assigned to patrol inside a public building at night has observed two men standing outside the doorway. Of the following, the MOST appropriate action for the officer to take FIRST is to

    A. approach the two men and ask them why they are standing there
    B. hide and wait for the two men to take some action
    C. phone the local police station and ask for help since these men may be planning criminal action
    D. check all the entrance doors of the building to make sure that they are locked

40. It is standard practice for special officers to inspect the restrooms in public buildings. This is done at regular intervals while on patrol.
    Of the following, the BEST reason for this practice is to

    A. inspect sanitary conditions
    B. discourage loiterers and potential criminals

C. check the ventilation
D. determine if all the equipment and plumbing is working properly

41. While on duty in the evening as an officer assigned to a public building, you receive a report that a card game is going on in one of the offices. Gambling is forbidden on government property.
Of the following, the BEST course of action for you to take is to

   A. go to the office and order the card players to leave
   B. ignore the complaint since this is probably just harmless social card playing
   C. report the matter to the building manager the next day
   D. go to the office and, if warranted, issue an appropriate warning

42. It has been suggested that special officers establish good working relationships with the local police officers of the police department on duty in the neighborhood.
Of the following, the MOST valid reason for this practice is that

   A. a spirit of good feeling and high morale will be created among members of the police department
   B. local police officers will probably cooperate more readily with the special officer
   C. local police officers can take over the building patrol duties of the special officer in case he is absent
   D. special officers have an even stronger obligation than ordinary citizens to cooperate with the police

43. It has been proposed that an officer assigned to a public building at night remain at one location in the building, instead of walking on patrol through the building.
This proposal is

   A. *bad;* chiefly because the officer would probably sit instead of stand at the proper location
   B. *good;* chiefly because the officer could do a better job of watching the entire building from one point
   C. *bad;* chiefly because anyone seeking to enter the building for illegal purposes might be able to do so at a point other than where the special officer is on duty
   D. *good;* chiefly because his supervisors would know exactly where to find him

44. In a busy office, an officer has been assigned the duty of making sure that the public is served in the order of their arrival at the office and that some employee is always taking care of a person desiring help.
Of the following, the BEST method for the officer to follow is to

   A. line up the persons in the waiting room
   B. give a numbered ticket to each person waiting and call out the numbers, in order, when an employee becomes available
   C. loudly announce "next" when an employee is available to serve someone
   D. seat one person next to each employee's desk and let the others wait for the first vacant seat

45. Two men have broken into and entered a building at night. The officer on duty at this building sees them, chases them out, and then observes them in the adjoining building.
   Of the following, the BEST course of action for the officer to take is to

   A. notify the local police station and be ready to aid the police
   B. enter the adjoining building to find the men
   C. notify the manager of his own building
   D. continue on duty since these men have left the building for which he is responsible

46. While an officer is on duty in a crowded waiting room, he finds a woman's purse on the floor.
   Of the following, the FIRST course of action for him to take is to

   A. hold it up in the air, ask who owns it, and give it to whoever claims it
   B. keep the purse until someone claims it
   C. immediately deliver the purse to the "lost and found" desk
   D. ask the lady who is nearest to him if she lost a purse

47. Special officers often have the power of arrest.
   Of the following, the BEST reason for this practice is to

   A. have the officer always arrest any person who refuses to obey his orders
   B. aid in maintaining order in places where he is assigned
   C. promote good public relations
   D. aid in preventing illegal use of public buildings by tenants or employees

48. An officer has told a mother that he found her son writing on the walls of the building with chalk. The mother tells the officer that he should be more concerned with "crooks" than with children's minor pranks.
   Of the following, the BEST answer for the officer to make to this woman is that

   A. children should be taught good conduct by their parents
   B. damage to public property means higher taxes
   C. serious criminals often begin their careers with minor violations
   D. it is his duty to enforce all rules and regulations

49. A man asks you, a special officer, where to get a certain kind of license not issued in your office. You don't know where such licenses are issued.
   Of the following, the BEST procedure for you to follow is to

   A. refer him to the manager of the office
   B. get the information if you can and give it to the man
   C. tell the man to inquire at any police station house
   D. tell the man that you just do not know

50. Special officers are not permitted to ask private citizens to buy tickets for dances or other such social functions, not even when such functions are operated by charitable organizations. Of the following, the BEST reason for this rule is that

   A. private citizens are under no obligation to buy any such tickets
   B. not all groups are allowed equal opportunity in the sale of their tickets
   C. private citizens might complain to officials
   D. private citizens might feel they would not get proper service unless they bought such tickets

KEY (CORRECT ANSWERS)

1. B	11. D	21. B	31. A	41. D
2. C	12. B	22. B	32. C	42. B
3. B	13. C	23. D	33. D	43. C
4. D	14. A	24. C	34. C	44. B
5. A	15. A	25. A	35. B	45. A
6. A	16. D	26. B	36. D	46. C
7. C	17. C	27. A	37. D	47. B
8. A	18. C	28. C	38. C	48. D
9. B	19. A	29. B	39. D	49. B
10. A	20. B	30. D	40. B	50. D

SOLUTIONS TO ARITHMETIC PROBLEMS

11. $2\frac{1}{4}$ miles are completed in 1 1/2 minutes (1 minute and 30 seconds)

$$\therefore 2\frac{1}{4} \div 1\frac{1}{2} = \text{rate per minute}$$

$$= \frac{9}{4} \div 1\frac{1}{2}$$

$$= \frac{9}{4} \div \frac{3}{2}$$

$$= \frac{9}{4} \times \frac{2}{3}$$

$$= \frac{3}{2} \text{ miles per minute}$$

$$\therefore \frac{3}{2} \times 60 \text{ (minutes in an hour)} = \text{rate per hour} = 90 \text{ miles per hour}$$

(Ans. D)

12. 550 + 2230 = 2780; 21,500 - 2780 = 18,720 passengers

550 buses at $14.00	=	$ 7,700
2230 trucks at $7.00	=	15,610
18720 passengers at $3.50	=	65,520
		$88,830

    (Ans. B)

13. Given: speed = 100 feet the first second

100 - 10 (10% of 100)	=	90 feet - the second second
90 - 9 (10% of 90)	=	81 feet - the third second
81 - 8.1 (10% of 81)	=	72.9 feet - the fourth second
		343.9 (total at end of the fourth second)

    (Ans. C)

14. Given: 500 = uniform allowance

    $500 - 180 = $320 (amount left after buying winter jacket)
    $320 x 40% = $128 (amount spent for two pairs of trousers)
    $320 - 128 = $192 (amount now left)

    Since the winter overcoat costs $240, he is now short $48 ($240 - 192) or 20% of the purchase price of the overcoat. ($48/240 = \frac{1}{5} = 20\%$)

(Ans. A)

15. Light cars: 9000(miles)÷30(miles per gallon)×3.75(per gallon)

$$= \frac{9000}{30} \times 3.75$$
$$= 300 \times 3.75$$
$$= \$1,125 \text{ (total gasoline cost)}$$

Standard cars: 9000 (miles) ÷ 15 (miles per gallon) x 3.75

$$= \frac{9000}{15} \times 3.75$$
$$= 600 \times 3.75$$
$$= \$2,250 \text{ (total gasoline cost)}$$

∴ use of light car would result in a saving in gasoline costs of $1,125 ($2,250 - $1,125).

(Ans. A)

16.
```
2006:   14,200     (burglary)
2005:   12,800     (burglary)
         1,400     (increase in burglaries)

2006:   34,750     (felony)
2005:   32,300     (felony)
         2,450     (increase in felonies
```

$$\therefore 1400 \div 2450 = \frac{1400}{2450} = .57$$

WORK

```
          .57
2450)1400.0
     1225.0
      175.00
      171.50
```

(Ans. D)

17. Given: smaller office: grants permits to 40% of 1/3 of the total number of applicants (900)

larger office: grants permits to 60% of 2/3 of the total number of applicants (900)

Solving: smaller office: $.40 \times \frac{1}{3} \times 900 = 120$ permits

larger office: $.60 \times \frac{2}{3} \times 900 = \underline{360}$ permits
$\phantom{larger office: .60 \times \frac{2}{3} \times 900 = }480$ permits (total)

(Ans. C)

SCANNING MAPS

One section of the exam tests your ability to orient yourself within a given region on a map. Using the map accompanying questions 1 through 3, choose the best way of getting from one point to another.

The New Bridge is closed to traffic because it has a broken span.

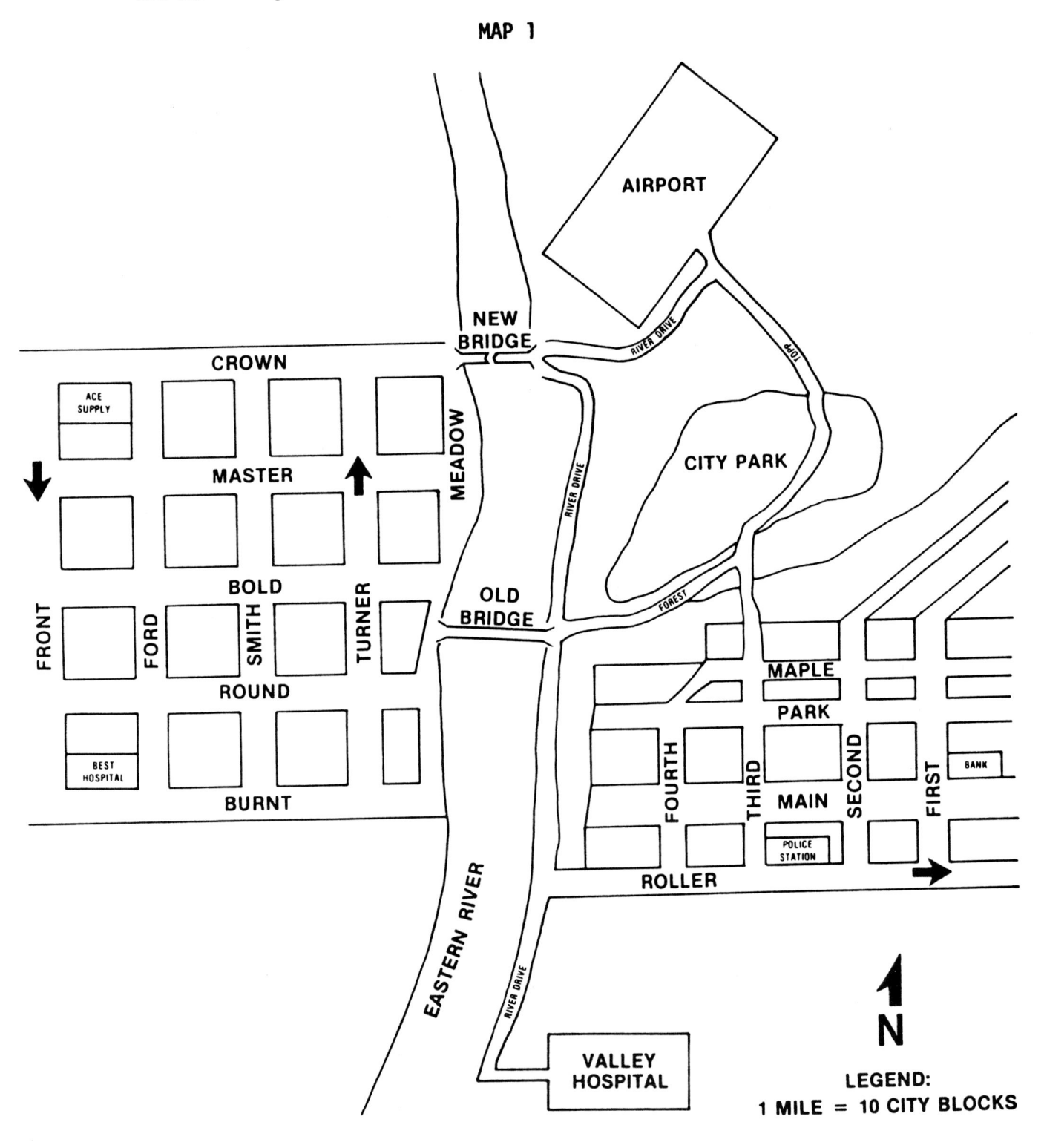

MAP 1

Arrows (⟶) indicate one-way traffic and direction of traffic. A street marked by an arrow is one way for the entire length of the street.

LEGEND: 1 MILE = 10 CITY BLOCKS

Sample Questions

1. Officers in a patrol car which is at the Airport receive a call for assistance at Best Hospital. The shortest route without breaking the law is:

   A. Southwest on River Drive, right on Forest, cross Old Bridge, south on Meadow, and west on Burnt to hospital entrance.
   B. Southwest on River Drive, right on New Bridge, left on Meadow, west on Burnt to hospital entrance.
   C. Southwest on River Drive, right on Old Bridge, left on Turner, right on Burnt to hospital entrance.
   D. North on River Drive to Topp, through City Park to Forest, cross Old Bridge, left on Meadow, west on Burnt to hospital entrance.

2. After returning to the police station, the officers receive a call to pick up injured persons at an accident site (located on the east side of New Bridge) and return to Valley Hospital. The shortest route without breaking the law is:

   A. West on Roller, north on River Drive, left to accident scene at New Bridge, then north on River Drive to hospital entrance.
   B. North on Third, left on Forest, north on River Drive, left to accident scene at new Bridge, then south on River Drive to hospital entrance.
   C. East on Roller, left on First, west on Maple, north on Third, left on Forest, north on River Drive to accident scene at New Bridge, then south on River Drive to hospital entrance.
   D. North on Third, left on Forest, cross Old Bridge, north on Meadow to New Bridge, south on Meadow, east over Old Bridge, then south on River Drive to hospital entrance.

3. While at the Valley Hospital, the officers receive a call asking them to pick up materials at the Ace Supply and return them to the police station. The shortest route without breaking the law is:

   A. North on River Drive, cross New Bridge, west on Crown to Ace Supply, then south on Front, east on Burnt, north on Meadow, cross Old Bridge, east on Forest, south on Third to police station.
   B. North on River Drive, right on Roller to police station, then north on Third, left on Forest, cross Old Bridge, north on Meadow, west on Crown to Ace Supply.
   C. North on River Drive, cross Old Bridge, north on Meadow, west on Crown to Ace Supply, then east on Crown, south on Meadow, cross Old Bridge, east on Forest, south on Third to police station.
   D. North on River Drive, cross Old Bridge, south on Meadow, west on Burnt, north on Front to Ace Supply, then east on Crown, south on Meadow, cross Old Bridge, east on Forest, south on Third to police station.

KEY (CORRECT ANSWERS)
1. A
2. B
3. C

EXAMINATION SECTION
TEST 1

DIRECTIONS: Each question or incomplete statement is followed by several suggested answers or completions. Select the one that BEST answers the question or completes the statement. *PRINT THE LETTER OF THE CORRECT ANSWER IN THE SPACE AT THE RIGHT.*

Questions 1-4.

DIRECTIONS: Questions 1 to 4 measure your ability (1) to determine whether statements from witnesses say essentially the same thing and (2) to determine the evidence needed to make it reasonably certain that a particular conclusion is true.

To do well in this part of the test, you do NOT have to have a working knowledge of police procedures and techniques or to have any more familiarity with crimes and criminal behavior than that acquired from reading newspapers, listening to radio, or watching TV. To do well in this part, you must read carefully and reason closely. Sloppy reading or sloppy reasoning will lead to a low score.

1. In which of the following do the two statements made say essentially the same thing in two different ways?
    I. All members of the pro-x group are free from persecution. No person that is persecuted is a member of the pro-x group.
    II. Some responsible employees of the police department are not supervisors. Some police department supervisors are not responsible employees.
    The CORRECT answer is:

    A. I *only* B. II *only*
    C. Both I and II D. Neither I nor II

2. In which of the following do the two statements made say essentially the same thing in two different ways?
    I. All Nassau County police officers weigh less than 225 pounds.
    II. No police officer weighs more than 225 pounds.
    No police officer is an alcoholic. No alcoholic is a police officer.
    The CORRECT answer is:

    A. I *only* B. II *only*
    C. Both I and II D. Neither I nor II

3. Summary of Evidence Collected to Date: All pimps in the precinct own pink-colored cars and carry knives.
    Prematurely Drawn Conclusion: Any person in the precinct who carries a knife is a pimp.
    Which one of the following additional pieces of evidence, if any, would make it *reasonably certain* that the conclusion drawn is TRUE?

    A. Each person who carries a knife owns a pink-colored car.
    B. All persons who own pink-colored cars pimp.

C. No one who carries a knife has a vocation other than pimping.
D. None of these

4. Summary of Evidence Collected to Date:
   1. Some of the robbery suspects have served time as convicted felons.
   2. Some of the robbery suspects are female.

   Prematurely Drawn Conclusion: Some of the female suspects have never served time as convicted felons.

   Which one of the following additional pieces of evidence, if any, would make it *reasonably certain* that the conclusion drawn is TRUE?

   A. The number of female suspects is the same as the number of robbery suspects who have served time as convicted felons.
   B. The number of female suspects is smaller than the number of convicted felons.
   C. The number of suspects that have served time is smaller than the number of suspects that have been convicted of a felony.
   D. None of these

4._

Questions 5-8.

DIRECTIONS: Questions 5 to 8 measure your ability to orient yourself within a given section of a town, neighborhood, or particular area. Each of the questions describes a starting point and a destination. Assume that you are driving a patrol car in the area shown on the map accompanying the questions. Use the map as a basis for choosing the shortest way to get from one point to another without breaking the law.

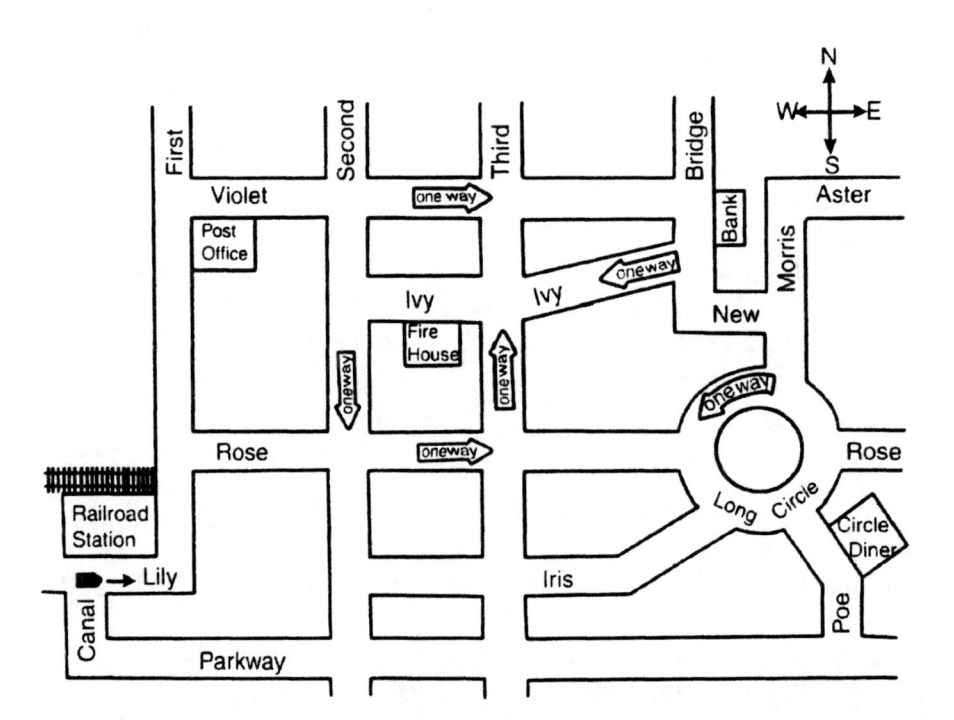

A street marked *one way* is one-way for the full length, even when there are breaks or jogs in the street. EXCEPTION: A street that does not have the same name over the full length.

5. A patrol car at the train station is sent to the bank to investigate a robbery. The SHORT-   5.____
   EST way to get there without breaking any traffic laws is to go

   A. east on Lily, north on First, east on Rose, north on Third, and east on Ivy to bank
   B. east on Lily, north on First, east on Violet, and south on Bridge to bank
   C. south on Canal, east on Parkway, north on Poe, around Long Circle to Morris, west on New, and north on Bridge to bank
   D. south on Canal, east on Parkway, north on Third, and east on Ivy to bank

6. At the bank, the patrol car receives a call to hurry to the post office. The SHORTEST way   6.____
   to get there without breaking any traffic laws is to go

   A. west on Ivy, south on Second, west on Rose, and north on First to post office
   B. west on Ivy, south on Second, west on Rose, and south on First to post office
   C. south on Bridge, east on New, south on Morris, around Long Circle, south on Poe, west on Parkway, north on Canal, east on Lily, and north on First to post office
   D. north on Bridge, west on Violet, and south on First to post office.

7. On leaving the post office, the police officers decide to go to the Circle Diner. The   7.____
   SHORTEST way to get there without breaking any traffic laws is to go

   A. south on First, left on Rose, right on Second, left on Parkway, and right on Poe to diner
   B. south on First, left on Rose, around Long Circle, and right on Poe to diner
   C. south on First, left on Rose, right on Second, right on Iris, around Long Circle, and left on Poe to diner
   D. west on Violet, right on Bridge, right on New, right on Morris, around Long Circle, and left on Poe to diner

8. During lunch break, a fire siren sounds and the police officers rush to their patrol car and   8.____
   head for the fire-house. The SHORTEST way to get there without breaking any traffic laws is to go

   A. north on Poe, around Long Circle, west on Iris, north on Third, and west on Ivy to firehouse
   B. north on Poe, around Long Circle, north on Morris, west on New, north on Bridge, and west on Ivy to firehouse
   C. north on Poe, around Long Circle, west on Rose, north on Third, and west on Ivy to firehouse
   D. south on Poe, west on Parkway, north on Third, and east on Ivy to firehouse

Questions 9-13.

DIRECTIONS: Questions 9 to 13 measure your ability to understand written descriptions of events. Each question presents you with a description of an accident, a crime, or an event and asks you which of four drawings BEST represent it.

In the drawings, the following symbols are used (these symbols and their meanings will be repeated in the test):

A moving vehicle is represented by this symbol: (front) ◁ (rear)

A parked vehicle is represented by this symbol: (front) ◀ (rear)

A pedestrian or a bicyclist is represented by this symbol: •

The path and direction of travel of a vehicle or pedestrian is indicated by a solid line: ⟶

EXCEPTION: The path and direction of travel of each vehicle or person directly involved in a collision from the point of impact is indicated by a dotted line: --▶

9. A driver pulling out from between two parked cars on Magic is struck by a vehicle heading east which turns left onto Maple and flees.
Which of the following depicts the accident?

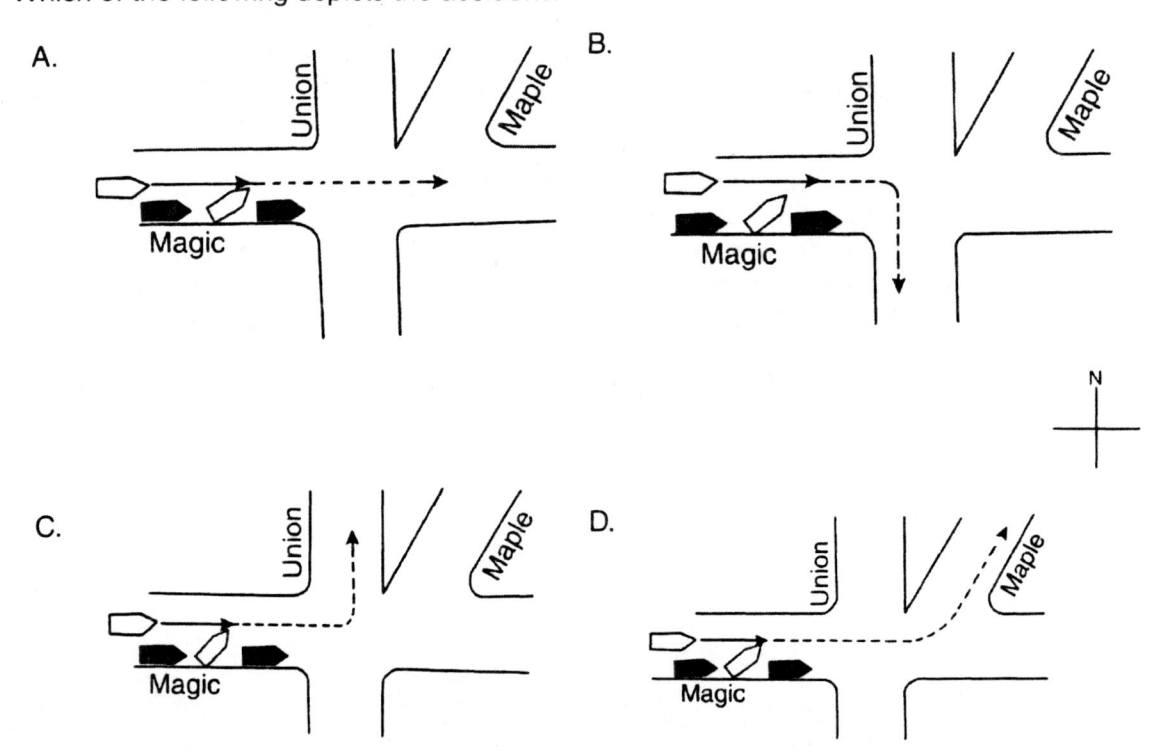

10. As Mr. Jones is driving south on Side. St., he falls asleep at the wheel. His car goes out of control and sideswipes an oncoming car, goes through an intersection, and hits a pedestrian on the southeast corner of Main Street.
Which of the following depicts the accident?

10.____

A.

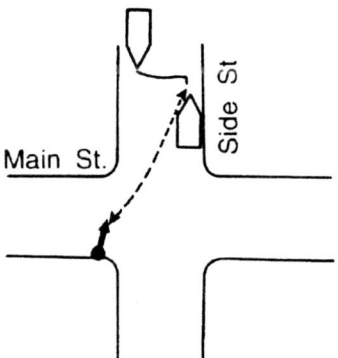

B.

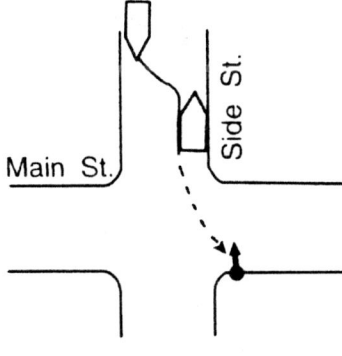

C.

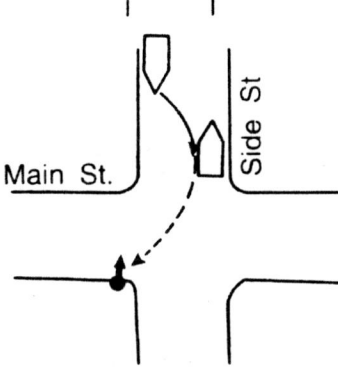

D.

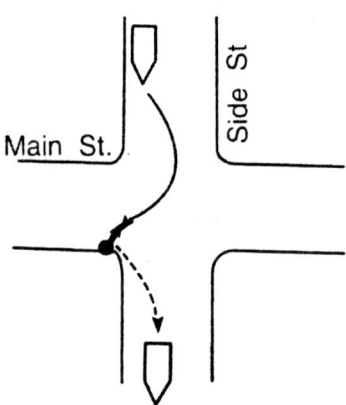

11. A car traveling south on Baltic skids through a red light at the intersection of Baltic and Atlantic, sideswipes a car stopped for a light in the northbound lane, skids 180 degrees, and stops on the west sidewalk of Baltic.
Which of the following depicts the accident?

11.____

A.

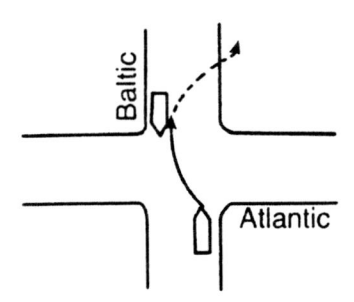

B.

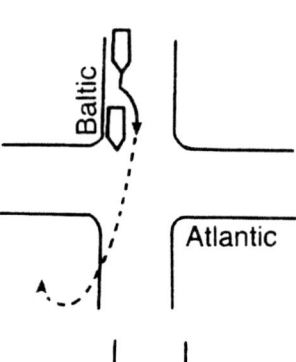

C.

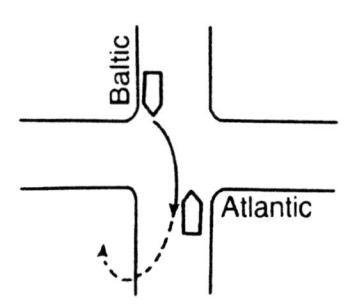

D.

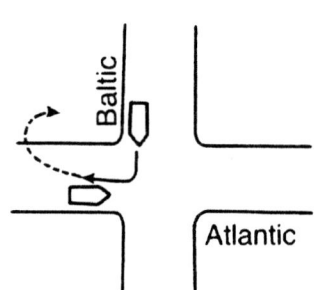

12. When found, the right front end of an automobile was smashed and bent around a post, and the hood was buckled.
Which of the following cars on a service lot is the car described?

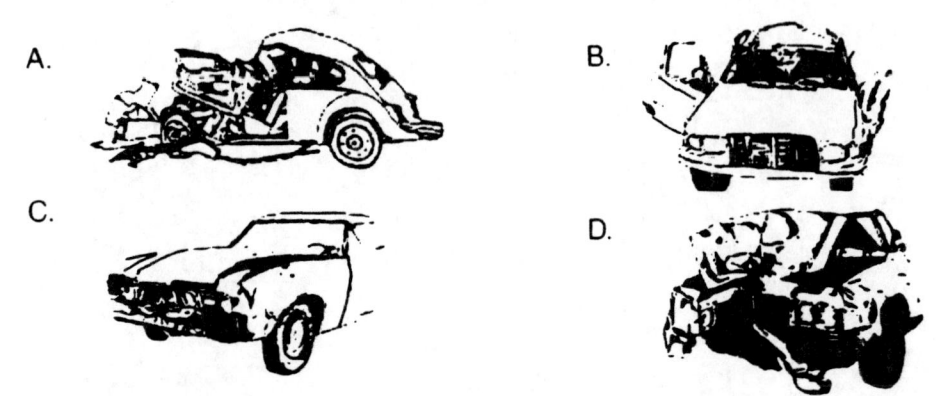

A.

B.

C.

D.

13. An open floor safe with its door bent out of shape was found at the scene. It was empty. An electric drill and several envelopes and papers were found on the floor near the safe.
Which of the following shows the scene described?

A.

B.

C.

D.

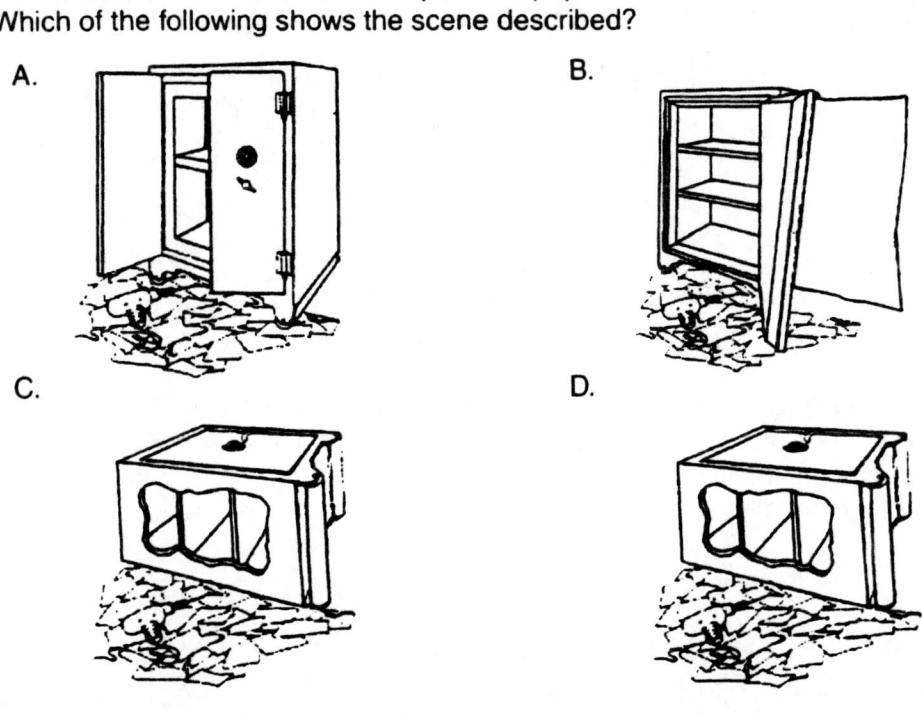

Questions 14-16.

DIRECTIONS: In Questions 14 to 16, you are to pick the word or phrase CLOSEST in meaning to the word or phrase printed in capital letters.

14. HAZARDOUS
 A. uncertain   B. threatening   C. difficult   D. dangerous

15. NEGLIGENT
 A. careless   B. fearless   C. ruthless   D. useless

16. PROVOKE
 A. accuse   B. arouse   C. insist   D. suspend

Questions 17-20.

DIRECTIONS: Questions 17 to 20 measure your ability to do arithmetic related to police work. Each question presents a separate arithmetic problem to be solved.

17. To the nearest hour, how long can a specialized police vehicle with a 40-gallon fuel tank be on the road before heading for a service facility, assuming that the vehicle consumes 8 gallons per hour and must head for a service facility when there are only 8 gallons in the tank?

   A. 3   B. 4   C. 5   D. None of these

18. A man with a history of vagrancy was found dead under a bridge with the following U.S. currency in a band around his belly:

   7   $5   bills
   3   $10 bills
   11 $20 bills
   9   $50 bills
   4   $100 bills

   What is the total amount of the money that was found in the band?

   A. $1,015   B. $1,135   C. $2,710   D. None of these

19. X is 110 dimes.
    Y is 1,111 pennies.
    Which of the following statements about the values of X and Y above is TRUE?

    A. X is greater than Y.
    B. Y is greater than X.
    C. X equals Y.
    D. The relationship of X to Y cannot be determined from the information given.

20. Which of the following individuals drinking hard liquor in a bar was 21 years old at the time of the incident?

    A. One born August 26, 1989 - Date of incident is March 17, 2010
    B. One born January 6, 1989 - Date of incident is New Year's Eve 2009
    C. One born 3/17/89 - Date of incident is 2/14/10
    D. None of these

KEY (CORRECT ANSWERS)

1.	A	11.	C
2.	B	12.	D
3.	C	13.	B
4.	D	14.	D
5.	B	15.	A
6.	C	16.	B
7.	B	17.	B
8.	B	18.	B
9.	D	19.	B
10.	B	20.	D

———

READING COMPREHENSION
UNDERSTANDING AND INTERPRETING WRITTEN MATERIAL

COMMENTARY

The ability to read, understand, and interpret written materials texts, publications, newspapers, orders, directions, expositions, legal passages is a skill basic to a functioning democracy and to an efficient business or viable government.

That is why almost all examinations – for beginning, middle, and senior levels – test reading comprehension, directly or indirectly.

The reading test measures how well you understand what you read. This is how it is done: You read a paragraph and several statements based on a question. From the statements, you choose the *one* statement, or answer, that is *BEST* supported by, or *BEST* matches, what is said in the paragraph.

SAMPLE QUESTIONS

DIRECTIONS: Each question has five suggested answers, lettered A, B, C, D, and E. Decide which one is the *BEST* answer. *PRINT THE LETTER OF THE CORRECT ANSWER IN THE SPACE AT THE RIGHT.*

1. The prevention of accidents makes it necessary not only that safety devices be used to guard exposed machinery but also that mechanics be instructed in safety rules which they must follow for their own protection and that the light in the plant be adequate.
   The paragraph BEST supports the statement that industrial accidents

   A. are always avoidable
   B. may be due to ignorance
   C. usually result from inadequate machinery
   D. cannot be entirely overcome
   E. result in damage to machinery

ANALYSIS

Remember what you have to do -
   First   -   Read the paragraph.
   Second -   Decide what the paragraph means.
   Third   -   Read the five suggested answers.
   Fourth -   Select the one answer which *BEST* matches what the paragraph says or is *BEST* supported by something in the paragraph. (Sometimes you may have to read the paragraph again in order to be sure which suggested answer is best.)

This paragraph is talking about three steps that should be taken to prevent industrial accidents:
   1. use safety devices on machines
   2. instruct mechanics in safety rules
   3. provide adequate lighting

SELECTION

With this in mind, let's look at each suggested answer. Each one starts with "Industrial accidents ..."

SUGGESTED ANSWER A.
Industrial accidents (A) are always avoidable.
(The paragraph talks about how to avoid accidents but does not say that accidents are always avoidable.)

SUGGESTED ANSWER B.
Industrial accidents (B) may be due to ignorance.
(One of the steps given in the paragraph to prevent accidents is to instruct mechanics on safety rules. This suggests that lack of knowledge or ignorance of safety rules causes accidents. This suggested answer sounds like a good possibility for being the right answer.)

SUGGESTED ANSWER C.
Industrial accidents (C) usually result from inadequate machinery.
(The paragraph does suggest that exposed machines cause accidents, but it doesn't say that it is the usual cause of accidents. The word *usually* makes this a wrong answer.)

SUGGESTED ANSWER D.
Industrial accidents (D) cannot be entirely overcome.
(You may know from your own experience that this is a true statement. But that is not what the paragraph is talking about. Therefore, it is NOT the correct answer.)

SUGGESTED ANSWER E.
Industrial accidents (E) result in damage to machinery.
(This is a statement that may or may not be true, but, in any case, it is NOT covered by the paragraph.)

Looking back, you see that the one suggested answer of the five given that *BEST* matches what the paragraph says is

Industrial accidents (B) may be due to ignorance.
The *CORRECT* answer then is B.
Be sure you read *ALL* the possible answers before you make your choice. You may think that none of the five answers is really good, but choose the *BEST* one of the five.

---

2. Probably few people realize, as they drive on a concrete road, that steel is used to keep the surface flat in spite of the weight of the busses and trucks. Steel bars, deeply embedded in the concrete, provide sinews to take the stresses so that the stresses cannot crack the slab or make it wavy.
The paragraph BEST supports the statement that a concrete road

A. is expensive to build
B. usually cracks under heavy weights
C. looks like any other road
D. is used only for heavy traffic
E. is reinforced with other material

ANALYSIS

This paragraph is commenting on the fact that -
1. few people realize, as they drive on a concrete road, that steel is deeply embedded
2. steel keeps the surface flat
3. steel bars enable the road to take the stresses without cracking or becoming wavy

SELECTION

Now read and think about the possible answers:
A. A concrete road is expensive to build.
   (Maybe so but that is not what the paragraph is about.)
B. A concrete road usually cracks under heavy weights.
   (The paragraph talks about using steel bars to prevent heavy weights from cracking concrete roads. It says nothing about how usual it is for the roads to crack. The word *usually* makes this suggested answer wrong.)
C. A concrete road looks like any other road.
   (This may or may not be true. The important thing to note is that it has nothing to do with what the paragraph is about.)
D. A concrete road is used only for heavy traffic.
   (This answer at least has something to do with the paragraph–concrete roads are used with heavy traffic but it does not say "used only.")
E. A concrete road is reinforced with other material.
   (This choice seems to be the correct one on two counts: *First*, the paragraph does suggest that concrete roads are made stronger by embedding steel bars in them. This is another way of saying "concrete roads are reinforced with steel bars." *Second*, by the process of elimination, the other four choices are ruled out as correct answers simply because they do not apply.)

You can be sure that not all the reading questions will be so easy as these.

SUGGESTIONS FOR ANSWERING READING QUESTIONS

1. Read the paragraph carefully. Then read each suggested answer carefully. Read every word, because often one word can make the difference between a right and a wrong answer.
2. Choose that answer which is supported in the paragraph itself. Do not choose an answer which is a correct statement unless it is based on information in the paragraph.
3. Even though a suggested answer has many of the words used in the paragraph, it may still be wrong.
4. Look out for words – such as *always, never, entirely, or only* – which tend to make a suggested answer wrong.

5. Answer first those questions which you can answer most easily. Then work on the other questions.
6. If you can't figure out the answer to the question, guess.

EXAMINATION SECTION
TEST 1

DIRECTIONS: The following questions are intended to test your ability to read with comprehension and to understand and interpret written materials, particularly legal passages. It will be necessary for you to read each paragraph carefully because the questions are based only on the material contained therein.
Each question has several suggested answers. *PRINT THE LETTER OF THE CORRECT ANSWER IN THE SPACE AT THE RIGHT.*

Questions 1-3.

DIRECTIONS: Answer Questions 1 to 3 *SOLELY* on the basis of the following statement:
Foot patrol has some advantages over all other methods of patrol. Maximum opportunity is provided for observation within range of the senses and for close contact with people and things that enable the patrolman to provide a maximum service as an information source and counselor to the public and as the eyes and ears of the police department. A foot patrolman loses no time in alighting from a vehicle, and the performance of police tasks is not hampered by responsibility for his vehicle while afoot. Foot patrol, however, does not have many of the advantages of a patrol car. Lack of both mobility and immediate communication with headquarters lessens the officer's value in an emergency. The area that he can cover effectively is limited and, therefore, this method of patrol is costly.

1. According to this paragraph, the foot patrolman is the eyes and ears of the police department because he is

    A. in direct contact with the station house
    B. not responsible for a patrol vehicle
    C. able to observe closely conditions on his patrol post
    D. a readily available information source to the public

1.____

2. The *MOST* accurate of the following statements concerning the various methods of patrol, according to this paragraph, is that

    A. foot patrol should sometimes be combined with motor patrol
    B. foot patrol is better than motor patrol
    C. helicopter patrol has the same advantages as motor patrol
    D. motor patrol is more readily able to communicate with superior officers in an emergency

2.____

3. According to this paragraph, it is *CORRECT* to state that foot patrol is

    A. *economical* since increased mobility makes more rapid action possible
    B. *expensive* since the area that can be patrolled is relatively small
    C. *economical* since vehicle costs need not be considered
    D. *expensive* since giving information to the public is time-consuming

3.____

Questions 4-6.

DIRECTIONS: Answer Questions 4 to 6 SOLELY on the basis of the following statement:
All applicants for an original license to operate a catering establishment shall be fingerprinted. This shall include the officers, employees, and stockholders of the company and the members of a partnership. In case of a change, by addition or substitution, occurring during the existence of a license, the person added or substituted shall be fingerprinted. However, in the case of a hotel containing more than 200 rooms, only the officer or manager filing the application is required to be fingerprinted. The police commissioner may also at his discretion exempt the employees and stockholders of any company. The fingerprints shall be taken on one copy of form C.E. 20 and on two copies of C.E. 21. One copy of form C.E. 21 shall accompany the application. Fingerprints are not required with a renewal application.

4. According to this paragraph, an employee added to the payroll of a licensed catering establishment which is not in a hotel, must

    A. always be fingerprinted
    B. be fingerprinted unless he has been previously fingerprinted for another license
    C. be fingerprinted unless exempted by the police commissioner
    D. be fingerprinted only if he is the manager or an officer of the company

5. According to this paragraph, it would be MOST accurate to state that

    A. form C.E. 20 must accompany a renewal application
    B. form C.E. 21 must accompany all applications
    C. form C.E. 21 must accompany an original application
    D. both forms C.E. 20 and C.E. 21 must accompany all applications

6. A hotel of 270 rooms has applied for a license to operate a catering establishment on the premises. According to the instructions for fingerprinting given in this paragraph, the

    A. officers, employees, and stockholders shall be fingerprinted
    B. officers and manager shall be fingerprinted
    C. employees shall be fingerprinted
    D. officer filing the application shall be fingerprinted

Questions 7-9.

DIRECTIONS: Answer Questions 7 to 9 SOLELY on the basis of the following statement:
It is difficult to instill in young people inner controls on aggressive behavior in a world marked by aggression. The slum child's environment, full of hostility, stimulates him to delinquency; he does that which he sees about him. The time to act against delinquency is before it is committed. It is clear that juvenile delinquency, especially when it is committed in groups or gangs, leads almost inevitably to an adult criminal life unless it is checked at once. The first signs of vandalism and disregard for the comfort, health, and property of the community should be considered as storm warnings which cannot be ignored. The delinquent's first crime has the underlying element of testing the law and its ability to hit back.

7. A *suitable* title for this entire paragraph based on the material it contains is: 7.____

    A. The Need for Early Prevention of Juvenile Delinquency
    B. Juvenile Delinquency as a Cause of Slums
    C. How Aggressive Behavior Prevents Juvenile Delinquency
    D. The Role of Gangs in Crime

8. According to this paragraph, an *INITIAL* act of juvenile crime *usually* involves a(n) 8.____

    A. group or gang activity
    B. theft of valuable property
    C. test of the strength of legal authority
    D. act of physical violence

9. According to this paragraph, acts of juvenile delinquency are *most likely* to lead to a criminal career when they are 9.____

    A. acts of vandalism
    B. carried out by groups or gangs
    C. committed in a slum environment
    D. such as to impair the health of the neighborhood

Questions 10-12.

DIRECTIONS: Answer Questions 10 to 12 *SOLELY* on the basis of the following statement:
The police laboratory performs a valuable service in crime investigation by assisting in the reconstruction of criminal action and by aiding in the identification of persons and things. When studied by a technician, physical things found at crime scenes often reveal facts useful in identifying the criminal and in determining what has occurred. The nature of substances to be examined and the character of the examinations to be made vary so widely that the services of a large variety of skilled scientific persons are needed in crime investigations. To employ such a complete staff and to provide them with equipment and standards needed for all possible analyses and comparisons is beyond the means and the needs of any but the largest police departments. The search of crime scenes for physical evidence also calls for the services of specialists supplied with essential equipment and assigned to each tour of duty so as to provide service at any hour.

10. If a police department employs a large staff of technicians of various types in its laboratory, it will affect crime investigation to the extent that 10.____

    A. most crimes will be speedily solved
    B. identification of criminals will be aided
    C. search of crime scenes for physical evidence will become of less importance
    D. investigation by police officers will not usually be required

11. According to this paragraph, the *MOST* complete study of objects found at the scenes of crimes is 11.____

    A. always done in all large police departments
    B. based on assigning one technician to each tour of duty
    C. probably done only in large police departments
    D. probably done in police departments of communities with low crime rates

12. According to this paragraph, a large variety of skilled technicians is useful in criminal investigations because

    A. crimes cannot be solved without their assistance as a part of the police team
    B. large police departments need large staffs
    C. many different kinds of tests on various substances can be made
    D. the police cannot predict what methods may be tried by wily criminals

Questions 13-14.

DIRECTIONS: Answer Questions 13 and 14 SOLELY on the basis of the following statement:
The emotionally unstable person is always potentially a dangerous criminal, who causes untold misery to other persons and is a source of considerable trouble and annoyance to law enforcement officials. Like his fellow criminals he will be a menace to society as long as he is permitted to be at large. Police activities against him serve to sharpen his wits, and imprisonment gives him the opportunity to learn from others how to commit more serious crimes when he is released. This criminal's mental structure makes it impossible for him to profit by his experience with the police officials, by punishment of any kind or by sympathetic understanding and treatment by well-intentioned persons, professional and otherwise.

13. According to the above paragraph, the MOST accurate of the following statements concerning the relationship between emotional instability and crime is that

    A. emotional instability is proof of criminal activities
    B. the emotionally unstable person can become a criminal
    C. all dangerous criminals are emotionally unstable
    D. sympathetic understanding will prevent the emotionally unstable person from becoming a criminal

14. According to the above paragraph, the effect of police activities on the emotionally unstable criminal is that

    A. police activities aid this type of criminal to reform
    B. imprisonment tends to deter this type of criminal from committing future crimes
    C. contact with the police serves to assist sympathetic understanding and medical treatment
    D. police methods against this type of criminal develop him for further unlawful acts

Questions 15-17.

DIRECTIONS: Answer Questions 15 to 17 SOLELY on the basis of the following statement:
Proposals to license gambling operations are based on the belief that the human desire to gamble cannot be suppressed and, therefore, it should be licensed and legalized with the people sharing in the profits, instead of allowing the underworld to benefit. If these proposals are sincere, then it is clear that only one is worthwhile at all. Legalized gambling should be completely controlled and operated by the state with all the profits used for its citizens. A state agency should be set up to operate and control the gambling business. It should be as completely removed from politics as possible. In view of the inherent nature of the gambling business, with its close relationship to lawlessness and crime, only a man of the highest integrity should be eligible to become head of this agency. However, state gambling would encourage mass gambling with its attending social and economic evils in the same manner as other forms of legal gambling; but there is no justification whatever for the business of gambling to be legalized and then permitted to operate for private profit or for the benefit of any political organization.

15. The CENTRAL thought of this paragraph may be *correctly* expressed as the   15._____

   A. need to legalize gambling in the state
   B. state operation of gambling for the benefit of the people
   C. need to license private gambling establishments
   D. evils of gambling

16. According to this paragraph, a problem of legalized gambling which will *still* occur if the state operates the gambling business is   16._____

   A. the diversion of profits from gambling to private use
   B. that the amount of gambling will tend to diminish
   C. the evil effects of any form of mass gambling
   D. the use of gambling revenues for illegal purposes

17. According to this paragraph, to legalize the business of gambling would be   17._____

   A. *justified* because gambling would be operated only by a man of the highest integrity
   B. *justified* because this would eliminate politics
   C. *unjustified* under any conditions because the human desire to gamble cannot be suppressed
   D. *unjustified* if operated for private or political profit

Questions 18-20.

DIRECTIONS: Answer Questions 18 to 20 SOLELY on the basis of the following statement:
   Whenever, in the course of the performance of their duties in an emergency, members of the force operate the emergency power switch at any location on the transit system and thereby remove power from portions of the track, or they are on the scene where this has been done, they will bear in mind that, although power is removed, further dangers exist; namely, that a train may coast into the area even though the power is off, or that the rails may be energized by a train which may be in a position to transfer electricity from a live portion of the third rail through its shoe beams. Employees must look in each direction before stepping upon, crossing, or standing close to tracks, being particularly careful not to come into contact with the third rail.

18. According to this paragraph, whenever an emergency occurs which has resulted in operating the emergency power switch, it is MOST accurate to state that   18._____

   A. power is shut off and employees may perform their duties in complete safety
   B. there may still be power in a portion of the third rail
   C. the switch will not operate if a portion of the track has been broken
   D. trains are not permitted to stop in the area of the emergency

19. An *important* precaution which this paragraph urges employees to follow after operating the emergency power switch, is to   19._____

   A. look carefully in both directions before stepping near the rails
   B. inspect the nearest train which has stopped to see if the power is on
   C. examine the third rail to see if the power is on
   D. check the emergency power switch to make sure it has operated properly

20. A trackman reports to you, a patrolman, that a dead body is lying on the road bed. You operate the emergency power switch. A train which has been approaching comes to a stop near the scene.
In order to act in accordance with the instructions in the above paragraph, you *should*

   A. climb down to the road bed and remove the body
   B. direct the train motorman to back up to the point where his train will not be in position to transfer electricity through its shoe beams
   C. carefully cross over the road bed to the body, avoiding the third rail and watching for train movements
   D. have the train motorman check to see if power is on before crossing to the tracks

21. The treatment to be given the offender cannot alter the fact of his offense; but we can take measures to reduce the chances of similar acts in the future. We should banish the criminal, not in order to exact revenge nor directly to encourage reform, but to deter him and others from further illegal attacks on society.
According to this paragraph, the *PRINCIPAL* reason for punishing criminals is to

   A. prevent the commission of future crimes
   B. remove them from society
   C. avenge society
   D. teach them that crime does not pay

22. Even the most comprehensive and best substantiated summaries of the total volume of criminal acts would not contribute greatly to an understanding of the varied social and biological factors which are sometimes assumed to enter into crime causation, nor would they indicate with any degree of precision the needs of police forces in combating crime.
According to this statement,

   A. crime statistics alone do not determine the needs of police forces in combating crime
   B. crime statistics are essential to a proper understanding of the social factors of crime
   C. social and biological factors which enter into crime causation have little bearing on police needs
   D. a knowledge of the social and biological factors of crime is essential to a proper understanding of crime statistics

23. The policeman's art consists of applying and enforcing a multitude of laws and ordinances in such degree or proportion and in such manner that the greatest degree of social protection will be secured. The degree of enforcement and the method of application will vary with each neighborhood and community.
According to the foregoing paragraph,

   A. each neighborhood or community must judge for itself to what extent the law is to be enforced
   B. a policeman should only enforce those laws which are designed to give the greatest degree of social protection
   C. the manner and intensity of law enforcement is not necessarily the same in all communities
   D. all laws and ordinances must be enforced in a community with the same degree of intensity

24. Police control in the sense of regulating the details of police operations, involves such matters as the technical means for so organizing the available personnel that competent police leadership, when secured, can operate effectively. It is concerned not so much with the extent to which popular controls can be trusted to guide and direct the course of police protection as with the administrative relationships which should exist between the component parts of the polie organism. According to the foregoing statement, police control is

    A. solely a matter of proper personnel assignment
    B. the means employed to guide and direct the course of police protection
    C. principally concerned with the administrative relationships between units of a police organization
    D. the sum total of means employed in rendering police protection

24.____

25. Police Department Rule 5 states that a Deputy Commissioner acting as Police Commissioner shall carry out the orders of the Police Commissioner, previously given, and such orders shall not, except in cases of extreme emergency, be countermanded. This means, most nearly, that, except in cases of extreme emergency,

    A. the orders given by a Deputy Commissioner acting as Police Commissioner may not be revoked
    B. a Deputy Commissioner acting as Police Commissioner should not revoke orders previously given by the Police Commissioner
    C. a Deputy Commissioner acting as Police Commissioner is vested with the same authority to issue orders as the Police Commissioner himself
    D. only a Deputy Commissioner acting as Police Commissioner may issue orders in the absence of the Police Commissioner himself

25.____

KEY (CORRECT ANSWERS)

1. C
2. D
3. B
4. C
5. C

6. D
7. A
8. C
9. B
10. B

11. C
12. C
13. B
14. D
15. B

16. C
17. D
18. B
19. A
20. C

21. A
22. A
23. C
24. C
25. B

TEST 2

Questions 1-2.

DIRECTIONS: Answer Questions 1 and 2 SOLELY on the basis of the following statement:
The medical examiner may contribute valuable data to the investigator of fires which cause fatalities. By careful examination of the bodies of any victims, he not only establishes cause of death, but may also furnish, in many instances, answers to questions relating to the identity of the victim and the source and origin of the fire. The medical examiner is of greatest value to law enforcement agencies because he is able to determine the exact cause of death through an examination of tissue of apparent arson victims. Thorough study of a burned body or even of parts of a burned body will frequently yield information which illuminates the problems confronting the arson investigator and the police.

1. According to the above paragraph, the MOST important task of the medical examiner in the investigation of arson is to obtain information concerning the

    A. identity of arsonists
    B. cause of death
    C. identity of victims
    D. source and origin of fires

2. The CENTRAL thought of the above paragraph is that the medical examiner aids in the solution of crimes of arson when

    A. a person is burnt to death
    B. identity of the arsonist is unknown
    C. the cause of the fire is known
    D. trained investigators are not available

Questions 3-6.

DIRECTIONS: Answer Questions 3 to 6 SOLELY on the basis of the following statement:
A foundling is an abandoned child whose identity is unknown. Desk officers shall direct the delivery, by a policewoman, if available, of foundlings actually or apparently under two years of age, to the Foundling Hospital, or if actually or apparently two years of age or over, to the Children's Center. In all other cases of dependent or neglected children, other than foundlings, requiring shelter, desk officers shall provide for obtaining such shelter as follows: between 9 a.m. and 5 p.m., Monday through Friday, by telephone direct to the Bureau of Child Welfare, in order to ascertain the shelter to which the child shall be sent; at all other times, direct the delivery of a child actually or apparently under two years of age to the Foundling Hospital, or, if the child is actually or apparently two years of age or over, to the Children's Center.

3. According to this paragraph, it would be MOST correct to state that

    A. a foundling as well as a neglected child may be delivered to the Foundling Hospital
    B. a foundling but not a neglected child may be delivered to the Children's Center
    C. a neglected child requiring shelter, regardless of age, may be delivered to the Bureau of Child Welfare
    D. the Bureau of Child Welfare may determine the shelter to which a foundling may be delivered

4. According to this paragraph, the desk officer shall provide for obtaining shelter for a neglected child, apparently under two years of age, by

   A. directing its delivery to the Children's Center if occurrence is on a Monday between 9 a.m. and 5 p.m.
   B. telephoning the Bureau of Child Welfare if occurrence is on a Sunday
   C. directing its delivery to the Foundling Hospital if occurrence is on a Wednesday at 4 p.m.
   D. telephoning the Bureau of Child Welfare if occurrence is at 10 a.m. on a Friday

5. According to this paragraph, the desk officer should direct delivery to the Foundling Hospital of any child who is

   A. actually under 2 years of age and requires shelter
   B. apparently under two years of age and is neglected or dependent
   C. actually 2 years of age and is a foundling
   D. apparently under 2 years of age and has been abandoned

6. A 12-year-old neglected child requiring shelter is brought to a police station on Thursday at 2 p.m. Such a child should be sent to

   A. a shelter selected by the Bureau of Child Welfare
   B. a shelter selected by the desk officer
   C. the Children's Center
   D. the Foundling Hospital when a brother or sister, under 2 years of age, also requires shelter

Questions 7-9.

DIRECTIONS: Answer Questions 7 to 9 SOLELY on the basis of the following statement:
In addition to making the preliminary investigation of crimes, patrolmen should serve as eyes, ears, and legs for the detective division. The patrol division may be used for surveillance, to serve warrants and bring in suspects and witnesses, and to perform a number of routine tasks for the detectives which will increase the time available for tasks that require their special skills and facilities. It is to the advantage of individual detectives, as well as of the detective division, to have patrolmen working in this manner; more cases are cleared by arrest and a greater proportion of stolen property is recovered when, in addition to the detective regularly assigned, a number of patrolmen also work on the case. Detectives may stimulate the interest and participation of patrolmen by keeping them currently informed of the presence, identity, or description, hangouts, associates, vehicles and method of operation of each criminal known to be in the community.

7. According to this paragraph, a patrolman should

   A. assist the detective in certain of his routine functions
   B. be considered for assignment as a detective on the basis of his patrol performance
   C. leave the scene once a detective arrives
   D. perform as much of the detective's duties as time permits

8. According to this paragraph, patrolmen should aid detectives by

   A. accepting assignments from detectives which give promise of recovering stolen property
   B. making arrests of witnesses for the detective's interrogation
   C. performing all special investigative work for detectives
   D. producing for questioning individuals who may aid the detective in his investigation

9. According to this paragraph, detectives can keep patrolmen interested by

   A. ascertaining that patrolmen are doing investigative work properly
   B. having patrolmen directly under his supervision during an investigation
   C. informing patrolmen of the value of their efforts in crime prevention
   D. supplying the patrolmen with information regarding known criminals in the community

Questions 10-11.

DIRECTIONS: Answer Questions 10 and 11 SOLELY on the basis of the following statement:
State motor vehicle registration departments should and do play a vital role in the prevention and detection of automobile thefts. The combatting of theft is, in fact, one of the primary purposes of the registration of motor vehicles. As of recent date, there were approximately 61,309,000 motor vehicles registered in the United States. That same year some 200,000 of them were stolen. All but 6 percent have been or will be recovered. This is a very high recovery ratio compared to the percentage of recovery of other stolen personal property. The reason for this is that automobiles are carefully identified by the manufacturers and carefully registered by many of the states.

10. The CENTRAL thought of this paragraph is that there is a close relationship between the

    A. number of automobiles registered in the United States and the number stolen
    B. prevention of automobile thefts and the effectiveness of police departments in the United States
    C. recovery of stolen automobiles and automobile registration
    D. recovery of stolen automobiles and of other stolen property

11. According to this paragraph, the high recovery ratio for stolen automobiles is due to

    A. state registration and manufacturer identification of motor vehicles
    B. successful prevention of automobile thefts by state motor vehicle departments
    C. the fact that only 6% of stolen vehicles are not properly registered
    D. the high number of motor vehicles registered in the United States

Questions 12-15.

DIRECTIONS: Answer Questions 12 to 15 SOLELY on the basis of the following statement:
It is not always understood that the term "physical evidence" embraces any and all objects, living or inanimate. A knife, gun, signature, or burglar tool is immediately recognized as physical evidence. Less often is it considered that dust, microscopic fragments of all types, even an odor, may equally be physical evidence and often the most important of all. It is well established that the most useful types of physical evidence are generally microscopic in dimensions, that is, not noticeable by the eye and, therefore, most likely to be overlooked by

the criminal and by the investigator. For this reason, microscopic evidence persists for months or years after all other evidence has been removed and found inconclusive. Naturally, there are limitations to the time of collecting microscopic evidence as it may be lost or decayed. The exercise of judgment as to the possibility or profit of delayed action in collecting the evidence is a field in which the expert investigator should judge.

12. The *one* of the following which the above paragraph does *NOT* consider to be physical evidence is a

    A. criminal thought
    B. minute speck of dust
    C. raw onion smell
    D. typewritten note

13. According to the above paragraph, the re-checking of the scene of a crime

    A. is *useless* when performed years after the occurrence of the crime
    B. is *advisable* chiefly in crimes involving physical violence
    C. *may turn up* microscopic evidence of value
    D. *should be delayed* if the microscopic evidence is not subject to decay or loss

14. According to the above paragraph, the criminal investigator *should*

    A. give most of his attention to weapons used in the commission of the crime
    B. ignore microscopic evidence until a request is received from the laboratory
    C. immediately search for microscopic evidence and ignore the more visible objects
    D. realize that microscopic evidence can be easily overlooked

15. According to the above paragraph,

    A. a delay in collecting evidence must definitely diminish its value to the investigator
    B. microscopic evidence exists for longer periods of time than other physical evidence
    C. microscopic evidence is generally the most useful type of physical evidence
    D. physical evidence is likely to be overlooked by the criminal and by the investigator

Questions 16-18.

DIRECTIONS: Answer Questions 16 to 18 *SOLELY* on the basis of the following statement:
Sometimes, but not always, firing a gun leaves a residue of nitrate particles on the hands. This fact is utilized in the paraffin test which consists of applying melted paraffin and gauze to the fingers, hands, and wrists of a suspect until a cast of approximately 1/8 of an inch is built up. The heat of the paraffin causes the pores of the skin to open and release any particles embedded in them. The paraffin cast is then removed and tested chemically for nitrate particles. In addition to gunpowder, fertilizers, tobacco ashes, matches, and soot are also common sources of nitrates on the hands.

16. Assume that the paraffin test has been given to a person suspected of firing a gun and that nitrate particles have been found. It would be *CORRECT* to conclude that the suspect

    A. is guilty
    B. is innocent
    C. may be guilty or innocent
    D. is probably guilty

17. In testing for the presence of gunpowder particles on human hands, the characteristic of paraffin which makes it MOST serviceable is that it

    A. causes the nitrate residue left by a fired gun to adhere to the gauze
    B. is waterproof
    C. melts at a low temperature
    D. helps to distinguish between gunpowder nitrates and other types

18. According to the above paragraph, in the paraffin test, the nitrate particles are removed from the pores because the paraffin

    A. enlarges the pores   B. contracts the pores
    C. reacts chemically with nitrates   D. dissolves the particles

Questions 19-21.

DIRECTIONS: Answer Questions 19 to 21 SOLELY on the basis of the following statement:
Pickpockets operate most effectively when there are prospective victims in either heavily congested areas or in lonely places. In heavily populated areas, the large number of people about them covers the activities of these thieves. In lonely spots, they have the advantage of working unobserved. The main factor in the pickpocket's success is the selection of the "right" victim, A pickpocket's victim must, at the time of the crime, be inattentive, distracted, or unconscious. If any of these conditions exist, and if the pickpocket is skilled in his operations, the stage is set for a successful larceny. With the coming of winter, the crowds move southward—and so do most of the pickpockets. However, some pickpockets will remain in certain areas all year around. They will concentrate on theater districts, bus and railroad terminals, hotels or large shopping centers. A complete knowledge of the methods of this type of criminal and the ability to recognize them come only from long years of experience in performing patient surveillance and trailing of them. This knowledge is essential for the effective control and apprehension of this type of thief.

19. According to this paragraph, the pickpocket is LEAST likely to operate in a

    A. baseball park with a full capacity attendance
    B. station in an outlying area late at night
    C. moderately crowded dance hall
    D. over-crowded department store

20. According to this paragraph, the one of the following factors which is NOT necessary for the successful operation of the pickpocket is that

    A. he be proficient in the operations required to pick pockets
    B. the "right" potential victims be those who have been the subject of such a theft previously
    C. his operations be hidden from the view of others
    D. the potential victim be unaware of the actions of the pickpocket

21. According to this paragraph, it would be MOST correct to conclude that police officers who are successful in apprehending pickpockets

    A. are generalling those who have had lengthy experience in recognizing all types of criminals
    B. must, by intuition, be able to recognize potential "right" victims

C. must follow the pickpockets in their southward movement
D. must have acquired specific knowledge and skills in this field

Questions 22-23.

DIRECTIONS: Answer Questions 22 and 23 SOLELY on the basis of the following statement:
For many years, slums had been recognized as breeding disease, juvenile delinquency, and crime which not only threatened the health and welfare of the people who lived there, but also weakened the structure of society as a whole. As far back as 1834, a sanitary inspection report in the city pointed out the connection between insanitary, overcrowded housing and the spread of epidemics. Down through the years, evidence of slum-produced evils accumulated as the slums themselves continued to spread. This spread of slums was nationwide. Its symptoms and its ill effects were peculiar to no locality, but were characteristic of the country as a whole and imperiled the national welfare.

22. According to this paragraph, people who live in slum dwellings

    A. cause slums to become worse
    B. are threatened by disease and crime
    C. create bad housing
    D. are the chief source of crime in the country

23. According to this paragraph, the effects of juvenile delinquency and crime in slum areas were

    A. to destroy the structure of society
    B. noticeable in all parts of the country
    C. a chief cause of the spread of slums
    D. to spread insanitary conditions in the city

Questions 24-25.

DIRECTIONS: Questions 24 and 25 pertain to the following section of the Penal Law:
Section 1942. A person who, after having been three times convicted within this state, of felonies or attempts to commit felonies, or under the law of any other state, government or country, of crimes which if committed within this state would be felonious, commits a felony, other than murder, first or second degree, or treason, within this state, shall be sentenced upon conviction of such fourth, or subsequent, offense to imprisonment in a state prison for an indeterminate term the minimum of which shall be not less than the maximum term provided for first offenders for the crime for which the individual has been convicted, but, in any event, the minimum term upon conviction for a felony as the fourth, or subsequent, offense, shall be not less than fifteen years, and the maximum thereof shall be his natural life.

24. Under the terms of the above stated portion of Section 1942 of the Penal Law, a person must receive the increased punishment therein provided if

    A. he is convicted of a felony and has been three times previously convicted of felonies
    B. he has been three times previously convicted of felonies, regardless of the nature of his present conviction

C. his fourth conviction is for murder, first or second degree, or treason
D. he has previously been convicted three times of murder, first or second degree, or treason

25. Under the terms of the above stated portion of Section 1942 of the Penal Law, a person convicted of a felony for which the penalty is imprisonment for a term not to exceed ten years, and who has been three times previously convicted of felonies in this state, shall be sentenced to a term the *minimum* of which shall be

A. ten years
B. fifteen years
C. indeterminate
D. his natural life

KEY (CORRECT ANSWERS)

1.	B	11.	A
2.	A	12.	A
3.	A	13.	C
4.	D	14.	D
5.	D	15.	C
6.	A	16.	C
7.	A	17.	A
8.	D	18.	A
9.	D	19.	C
10.	C	20.	B

21. D
22. B
23. B
24. A
25. B

PREPARING WRITTEN MATERIAL

EXAMINATION SECTION
TEST 1

DIRECTIONS: Each question or incomplete statement is followed by several suggested answers or completions. Select the one that BEST answers the question or completes the statement. *PRINT THE LETTER OF THE CORRECT ANSWER IN THE SPACE AT THE RIGHT.*

Questions 1-4.

DIRECTIONS: Questions 1 through 4 each consist of a sentence which may or may not be an example of good English. The underlined parts of each sentence may be correct or incorrect. Examine each sentence, considering grammar, punctuation, spelling, and capitalization. If the English usage in the underlined parts of the sentence given is better than any of the changes in the underlined words suggested in options B, C, or D, choose option A. If the changes in the underlined words suggested in options B, C, or D would make the sentence correct, choose the correct option. Do not choose an option that will change the meaning of the sentence.

1. This <u>Fall</u>, the office will be closed on <u>Columbus Day, October</u> 9th. 1._____

   A. Correct as is
   B. fall...Columbus Day, October
   C. Fall...columbus day, October
   D. fall...Columbus Day, October

2. There <u>weren't no</u> paper in the supply closet. 2._____

   A. Correct as is B. weren't any
   C. wasn't any   D. wasn't no

3. The <u>alphabet, or A to Z sequence are</u> the basis of most filing systems. 3._____

   A. Correct as is
   B. alphabet, or A to Z sequence, is
   C. alphabet, or A to Z sequence, are
   D. alphabet, or A too Z sequence, is

4. The Office Aide checked the <u>register and finding</u> the date of the meeting. 4._____

   A. Correct as is   B. regaster and finding
   C. register and found   D. regaster and found

Questions 5-10.

DIRECTIONS: Questions 5 through 10 consist of sentences which contain examples of correct or incorrect English usage. Examine each sentence with reference to grammar, spelling, punctuation, and capitalization. Choose one of the following options that would be BEST for correct English usage:

A. The sentence is correct
B. There is one mistake
C. There are two mistakes
D. There are three mistakes

5. Mrs. Fitzgerald came to the 59th Precinct to retreive her property which were stolen earlier in the week. 5.____

6. The two officer's responded to the call, only to find that the perpatrator and the victim have left the scene. 6.____

7. Mr. Coleman called the 61st Precinct to report that, upon arriving at his store, he discovered that there was a large hole in the wall and that three boxes of radios were missing. 7.____

8. The Administrative Lieutenant of the 62nd Precinct held a meeting which was attended by all the civilians, assigned to the Precinct. 8.____

9. Three days after the robbery occured the detective apprahended two suspects and recovered the stolen items. 9.____

10. The Community Affairs Officer of the 64th Precinct is the liaison between the Precinct and the community; he works closely with various community organizations, and elected officials. 10.____

Questions 11-18.

DIRECTIONS: Questions 11 through 18 are to be answered on the basis of the following paragraph, which contains some deliberate errors in spelling and/or grammar and/or punctuation. Each line of the paragraph is preceded by a number. There are 9 lines and 9 numbers.

Line No.	Paragraph Line
1	The protection of life and property are, one of
2	the oldest and most important functions of a city.
3	New York city has it's own full-time police Agency.
4	The police Department has the power an it shall
5	be there duty to preserve the Public piece,
6	prevent crime detect and arrest offenders, supress
7	riots, protect the rites of persons and property, etc.
8	The maintainance of sound relations with the community they
9	serve is an important function of law enforcement officers

11. How many errors are contained in line one? 11.____
    A. One   B. Two   C. Three   D. None

12. How many errors are contained in line two? 12.____
    A. One   B. Two   C. Three   D. None

13. How many errors are contained in line three? 13.____
    A. One   B. Two   C. Three   D. None

14. How many errors are contained in line four? 14.____
    A. One   B. Two   C. Three   D. None

15. How many errors are contained in line five? 15.____
    A. One   B. Two   C. Three   D. None

16. How many errors are contained in line six? 16.____
    A. One   B. Two   C. Three   D. None

17. How many errors are contained in line seven? 17.____
    A. One   B. Two   C. Three   D. None

18. How many errors are contained in line eight? 18.____
    A. One   B. Two   C. Three   D. None

19. In the sentence, *The candidate wants to file his application for preference before it is too late,* the word *before* is used as a(n) 19.____

    A. preposition
    B. subordinating conjunction
    C. pronoun
    D. adverb

20. The one of the following sentences which is grammatically PREFERABLE to the others is: 20.____

    A. Our engineers will go over your blueprints so that you may have no problems in construction.
    B. For a long time he had been arguing that we, not he, are to blame for the confusion.
    C. I worked on this automobile for two hours and still cannot find out what is wrong with it.
    D. Accustomed to all kinds of hardships, fatigue seldom bothers veteran policemen.

KEY (CORRECT ANSWERS)

1.	A	11.	C
2.	C	12.	D
3.	B	13.	C
4.	C	14.	B
5.	C	15.	C
6.	D	16.	B
7.	A	17.	A
8.	C	18.	A
9.	C	19.	B
10.	B	20.	A

TEST 2

DIRECTIONS: Each question or incomplete statement is followed by several suggested answers or completions. Select the one that BEST answers the question or completes the statement. *PRINT THE LETTER OF THE CORRECT ANSWER IN THE SPACE AT THE RIGHT.*

1. The plural of 1.____

   A. turkey is turkies
   B. cargo is cargoes
   C. bankruptcy is bankruptcys
   D. son-in-law is son-in-laws

2. The abbreviation *viz.* means MOST NEARLY 2.____

   A. namely   B. for example
   C. the following   D. see

3. In the sentence, *A man in a light-grey suit waited thirty-five minutes in the ante-room for the all-important document,* the word IMPROPERLY hyphenated is 3.____

   A. light-grey   B. thirty-five
   C. ante-room   D. all-important

4. The MOST accurate of the following sentences is: 4.____

   A. The commissioner, as well as his deputy and various bureau heads, were present.
   B. A new organization of employers and employees have been formed.
   C. One or the other of these men have been selected.
   D. The number of pages in the book is enough to discourage a reader.

5. The MOST accurate of the following sentences is: 5.____

   A. Between you and me, I think he is the better man.
   B. He was believed to be me.
   C. Is it us that you wish to see?
   D. The winners are him and her.

Questions 6-13.

DIRECTIONS: The sentences numbered 6 through 13 deal with some phase of police activity. They may be classified most appropriately under one of the following four categories.
   A. Faulty because of incorrect grammar
   B. Faulty because of incorrect punctuation
   C. Faulty because of incorrect use of a word
   D. Correct

Examine each sentence carefully. Then, in the space at the right, print the capital letter preceding the option which is the BEST of the four suggested above. All incorrect sentences contain only one type of error. Consider a sentence correct if it contains none of the types of errors mentioned, even though there may be other correct ways of expressing the same thought.

6. The Department Medal of Honor is awarded to a member of the Police Force who distinguishes himself inconspicuously in the line of police duty by the performance of an act of gallantry.

7. Members of the Detective Division are charged with the prevention of crime, the detection and arrest of criminals and the recovery of lost or stolen property.

8. Detectives are selected from the uniformed patrol forces after they have indicated by conduct, aptitude and performance that they are qualified for the more intricate duties of a detective.

9. The patrolman, pursuing his assailant, exchanged shots with the gunman and immortaly wounded him as he fled into a nearby building.

10. The members of the Traffic Division has to enforce the Vehicle and Traffic Law, the Traffic Regulations and ordinances relating to vehicular and pedestrian traffic.

11. After firing a shot at the gunman, the crowd dispersed from the patrolman's line of fire.

12. The efficiency of the Missing Persons Bureau is maintained with a maximum of public personnel due to the specialized training given to its members.

13. Records of persons arrested for violations of Vehicle and Traffic Regulations are transmitted upon request to precincts, courts and other authorized agencies.

14. Following are two sentences which may or may not be written in correct English:
    I. Two clients assaulted the officer.
    II. The van is illegally parked.
    Which one of the following statements is CORRECT?

    A. Only Sentence I is written in correct English.
    B. Only Sentence II is written in correct English.
    C. Sentences I and II are both written in correct English.
    D. Neither Sentence I nor Sentence II is written in correct English.

15. Following are two sentences which may or may not be written in correct English:
    I. Security Officer Rollo escorted the visitor to the patrolroom.
    II. Two entry were made in the facility logbook.
    Which one of the following statements is CORRECT?

    A. Only Sentence I is written in correct English.
    B. Only Sentence II is written in correct English.
    C. Sentences I and II are both written in correct English.
    D. Neither Sentence I nor Sentence II is written in correct English.

16. Following are two sentences which may or may not be written in correct English:
    I. Officer McElroy putted out a small fire in the wastepaper basket.
    II. Special Officer Janssen told the visitor where he could obtained a pass.
    Which one of the following statements is CORRECT?

    A. Only Sentence I is written in correct English.
    B. Only Sentence II is written in correct English.
    C. Sentences I and II are both written in correct English.
    D. Neither Sentence I nor Sentence II is written in correct English.

17. Following are two sentences which may or may not be written in correct English:
    I. Security Officer Warren observed a broken window while he was on his post in Hallway C.
    II. The worker reported that two typewriters had been stoled from the office.
    Which one of the following statements is CORRECT?

    A. Only Sentence I is written in correct English.
    B. Only Sentence II is written in correct English.
    C. Sentences I and II are both written in correct English.
    D. Neither Sentence I nor Sentence II is written in correct English.

17._____

18. Following are two sentences which may or may not be written in correct English:
    I. Special Officer Cleveland was attempting to calm an emotionally disturbed visitor.
    II. The visitor did not stops crying and calling for his wife.
    Which one of the following statements is CORRECT?

    A. Only Sentence I is written in correct English.
    B. Only Sentence II is written in correct English.
    C. Sentences I and II are both written in correct English.
    D. Neither Sentence I nor Sentence II is written in correct English.

18._____

19. Following are two sentences that may or may not be written in correct English:
    I. While on patrol, I observes a vagrant loitering near the drug dispensary.
    II. I escorted the vagrant out of the building and off the premises.
    Which one of the following statements is CORRECT?

    A. Only Sentence I is written in correct English.
    B. Only Sentence II is written in correct English.
    C. Sentences I and II are both written in correct English.
    D. Neither Sentence I nor Sentence II is written in correct English.

19._____

20. Following are two sentences which may or may not be written in correct English:
    I. At 4:00 P.M., Sergeant Raymond told me to evacuate the waiting area immediately due to a bomb threat.
    II. Some of the clients did not want to leave the building.
    Which one of the following statements is CORRECT?

    A. Only Sentence I is written in correct English.
    B. Only Sentence II is written in correct English.
    C. Sentences I and II are both written in correct English.
    D. Neither Sentence I nor Sentence II is written in correct English.

20._____

KEY (CORRECT ANSWERS)

1. B
2. A
3. C
4. D
5. A

6. C
7. B
8. D
9. C
10. A

11. A
12. C
13. D
14. C
15. A

16. D
17. A
18. A
19. B
20. C

PREPARING WRITTEN MATERIAL

PARAGRAPH REARRANGEMENT
COMMENTARY

The sentences which follow are in scrambled order. You are to rearrange them in proper order and indicate the letter choice containing the correct answer at the space at the right.

Each group of sentences in this section is actually a paragraph presented in scrambled order. Each sentence in the group has a place in that paragraph; no sentence is to be left out. You are to read each group of sentences and decide upon the best order in which to put the sentences so as to form as well-organized paragraph.

The questions in this section measure the ability to solve a problem when all the facts relevant to its solution are not given.

More specifically, certain positions of responsibility and authority require the employee to discover connections between events sometimes, apparently, unrelated. In order to do this, the employee will find it necessary to correctly infer that unspecified events have probably occurred or are likely to occur. This ability becomes especially important when action must be taken on incomplete information.

Accordingly, these questions require competitors to choose among several suggested alternatives, each of which presents a different sequential arrangement of the events. Competitors must choose the MOST logical of the suggested sequences.

In order to do so, they may be required to draw on general knowledge to infer missing concepts or events that are essential to sequencing the given events. Competitors should be careful to infer only what is essential to the sequence. The plausibility of the wrong alternatives will always require the inclusion of unlikely events or of additional chains of events which are NOT essential to sequencing the given events.

It's very important to remember that you are looking for the best of the four possible choices, and that the best choice of all may not even be one of the answers you're given to choose from.

There is no one right way to these problems. Many people have found it helpful to first write out the order of the sentences, as they would have arranged them, on their scrap paper before looking at the possible answers. If their optimum answer is there, this can save them some time. If it isn't, this method can still give insight into solving the problem. Others find it most helpful to just go through each of the possible choices, contrasting each as they go along. You should use whatever method feels comfortable, and works, for you.

While most of these types of questions are not that difficult, we've added a higher percentage of the difficult type, just to give you more practice. Usually there are only one or two questions on this section that contain such subtle distinctions that you're unable to answer confidently, and you then may find yourself stuck deciding between two possible choices, neither of which you're sure about.

EXAMINATION SECTION
TEST 1

DIRECTIONS: Each question consists of several sentences which can be arranged in a logical sequence. For each question, select the choice which places the numbered sentences in the MOST logical sequence. *PRINT THE LETTER OF THE CORRECT ANSWER IN THE SPACE AT THE RIGHT.*

1.
    I. A body was found in the woods.
    II. A man proclaimed innocence.
    III. The owner of a gun was located.
    IV. A gun was traced.
    V. The owner of a gun was questioned.
    The CORRECT answer is:

    A. IV, III, V, II, I B. II, I, IV, III, V
    C. I, IV, III, V, II D. I, III, V, II, IV
    E. I, II, IV, III, V

    1.____

2.
    I. A man was in a hunting accident.
    II. A man fell down a flight of steps.
    III. A man lost his vision in one eye.
    IV. A man broke his leg.
    V. A man had to walk with a cane.
    The CORRECT answer is:

    A. II, IV, V, I, III B. IV, V, I, III, II
    C. III, I, IV, V, II D. I, III, V, II, IV
    E. I, III, II, IV, V

    2.____

3.
    I. A man is offered a new job.
    II. A woman is offered a new job.
    III. A man works as a waiter.
    IV. A woman works as a waitress.
    V. A woman gives notice.
    The CORRECT answer is:

    A. IV, II, V, III, I B. IV, II, V, I, III
    C. II, IV, V, III, I D. III, I, IV, II, V
    E. IV, III, II, V, I

    3.____

4.
    I. A train left the station late.
    II. A man was late for work.
    III. A man lost his job.
    IV. Many people complained because the train was late.
    V. There was a traffic jam.
    The CORRECT answer is:

    A. V, II, I, IV, III B. V, I, IV, II, III
    C. V, I, II, IV, III D. I, V, IV, II, III
    E. II, I, IV, V, III

    4.____

5.
I. The burden of proof as to each issue is determined before trial and remains upon the same party throughout the trial.
II. The jury is at liberty to believe one witness' testimony as against a number of contradictory witnesses.
III. In a civil case, the party bearing the burden of proof is required to prove his contention by a fair preponderance of the evidence.
IV. However, it must be noted that a fair preponderance of evidence does not necessarily mean a greater number of witnesses.
V. The burden of proof is the burden which rests upon one of the parties to an action to persuade the trier of the facts, generally the jury, that a proposition he asserts is true.
VI. If the evidence is equally balanced, or if it leaves the jury in such doubt as to be unable to decide the controversy either way, judgment must be given against the party upon whom the burden of proof rests.

The CORRECT answer is:

A. III, II, V, IV, I, VI
B. I, II, VI, V, III, IV
C. III, IV, V, I, II, VI
D. V, I, III, VI, IV, II
E. I, V, III, VI, IV, II

6.
I. If a parent is without assets and is unemployed, he cannot be convicted of the crime of non-support of a child.
II. The term *sufficient ability* has been held to mean sufficient financial ability.
III. It does not matter if his unemployment is by choice or unavoidable circumstances.
IV. If he fails to take any steps at all, he may be liable to prosecution for endangering the welfare of a child.
V. Under the penal law, a parent is responsible for the support of his minor child only if the parent is *of* sufficient ability.
VI. An indigent parent may meet his obligation by borrowing money or by seeking aid under the provisions of the Social Welfare Law.

The CORRECT answer is:

A. VI, I, V, III, II, IV
B. I, III, V, II, IV, VI
C. V, II, I, III, VI, IV
D. I, VI, IV, V, II, III
E. II, V, I, III, VI, IV

7.
I. Consider, for example, the case of a rabble rouser who urges a group of twenty people to go out and break the windows of a nearby factory.
II. Therefore, the law fills the indicated gap with the crime of *inciting to riot*.
III. A person is considered guilty of inciting to riot when he urges ten or more persons to engage in tumultuous and violent conduct of a kind likely to create public alarm.
IV. However, if he has not obtained the cooperation of at least four people, he cannot be charged with unlawful assembly.
V. The charge of inciting to riot was added to the law to cover types of conduct which cannot be classified as either the crime of *riot* or the crime of *unlawful assembly*.
VI. If he acquires the acquiescence of at least four of them, he is guilty of unlawful assembly even if the project does not materialize.

The CORRECT answer is:

A. III, V, I, VI, IV, II   B. V, I, IV, VI, II, III
C. III, IV, I, V, II, VI   D. V, I, IV, VI, III, II
E. V, III, I, VI, IV, II

8. I.   If, however, the rebuttal evidence presents an issue of credibility, it is for the jury to determine whether the presumption has, in fact, been destroyed.
    II. Once sufficient evidence to the contrary is introduced, the presumption disappears from the trial.
    III. The effect of a presumption is to place the burden upon the adversary to come forward with evidence to rebut the presumption.
    IV. When a presumption is overcome and ceases to exist in the case, the fact or facts which gave rise to the presumption still remain.
    V.   Whether a presumption has been overcome is ordinarily a question for the court.
    VI. Such information may furnish a basis for a logical inference.
    The CORRECT answer is:

    A. IV, VI, II, V, I, III   B. III, II, V, I, IV, VI
    C. V, III, VI, IV, II, I   D. V, IV, I, II, VI, III
    E. II, III, V, I, IV, VI

9. I.   An executive may answer a letter by writing his reply on the face of the letter itself instead of having a return letter typed.
    II. This procedure is efficient because it saves the executive's time, the typist's time, and saves office file space.
    III. Copying machines are used in small offices as well as large offices to save time and money in making brief replies to business letters.
    IV. A copy is made on a copying machine to go into the company files, while the original is mailed back to the sender.
    The CORRECT answer is:

    A. I, II, IV, III   B. I, IV, II, III
    C. III, I, IV, II   D. III, IV, II, I

10. I.   Most organizations favor one of the types but always include the others to a lesser degree.
    II. However, we can detect a definite trend toward greater use of symbolic control.
    III. We suggest that our local police agencies are today primarily utilizing material control.
    IV. Control can be classified into three types: physical, material, and symbolic.
    The CORRECT answer is:

    A. IV, II, III, I   B. II, I, IV, III
    C. III, IV, II, I   D. IV, I, III, II

11. I.   Project residents had first claim to this use, followed by surrounding neighborhood children.
    II. By contrast, recreation space within the project's interior was found to be used more often by both groups.
    III. Studies of the use of project grounds in many cities showed grounds left open for public use were neglected and unused, both by residents and by members of the surrounding community.

IV. Project residents had clearly laid claim to the play spaces, setting up and enforcing unwritten rules for use.
V. Each group, by experience, found their activities easily disrupted by other groups, and their claim to the use of space for recreation difficult to enforce.

The CORRECT answer is:

A. IV, V, I, II, III
B. V, II, IV, III, I
C. I, IV, III, II, V
D. III, V, II, IV, I

12.
I. They do not consider the problems correctable within the existing subsidy formula and social policy of accepting all eligible applicants regardless of social behavior and lifestyle.
II. A recent survey, however, indicated that tenants believe these problems correctable by local housing authorities and management within the existing financial formula.
III. Many of the problems and complaints concerning public housing management and design have created resentment between the tenant and the landlord.
IV. This same survey indicated that administrators and managers do not agree with the tenants.

The CORRECT answer is:

A. II, I, III, IV
B. I, III, IV, II
C. III, II, IV, I
D. IV, II, I, III

13.
I. In single-family residences, there is usually enough distance between tenants to prevent occupants from annoying one another.
II. For example, a certain small percentage of tenant families has one or more members addicted to alcohol.
III. While managers believe in the right of individuals to live as they choose, the manager becomes concerned when the pattern of living jeopardizes others' rights.
IV. Still others turn night into day, staging lusty entertainments which carry on into the hours when most tenants are trying to sleep.
V. In apartment buildings, however, tenants live so closely together that any misbehavior can result in unpleasant living conditions.
VI. Other families engage in violent argument.

The CORRECT answer is:

A. III, II, V, IV, VI, I
B. I, V, II, VI, IV, III
C. II, V, IV, I, III, VI
D. IV, II, V, VI, III, I

14.
I. Congress made the commitment explicit in the Housing Act of 1949, establishing as a national goal the realization of *a decent home and suitable environment for every American family.*
II. The result has been that the goal of decent home and suitable environment is still as far distant as ever for the disadvantaged urban family.
III. In spite of this action by Congress, federal housing programs have continued to be fragmented and grossly underfunded.
IV. The passage of the National Housing Act signalled a new federal commitment to provide housing for the nation's citizens.

The CORRECT answer is:

A. I, IV, III, II
B. IV, I, III, II
C. IV, I, II, III
D. II, IV, I, III

15.
   I. The greater expense does not necessarily involve *exploitation,* but it is often perceived as exploitative and unfair by those who are aware of the price differences involved, but unaware of operating costs.
   II. Ghetto residents believe they are *exploited* by local merchants, and evidence substantiates some of these beliefs.
   III. However, stores in low-income areas were more likely to be small independents, which could not achieve the economies available to supermarket chains and were, therefore, more likely to charge higher prices, and the customers were more likely to buy smaller-sized packages which are more expensive per unit of measure.
   IV. A study conducted in one city showed that distinctly higher prices were charged for goods sold in ghetto stores than in other areas.

   The CORRECT answer is:

   A. IV, II, I, III
   B. IV, I, III, II
   C. II, IV, III, I
   D. II, III, IV, I

15.____

KEY (CORRECT ANSWERS)

1. C
2. E
3. B
4. D
5. D

6. C
7. A
8. B
9. C
10. D

11. D
12. C
13. B
14. B
15. C

CAMPUS SECURITY OFFICER

The history of the campus security officer has involved a variety of services performed by numerous individuals classified under differing job descriptions. The watchman, the janitor, the guard, and various levels of faculty and administration, at different times and places, have each performed acts that are today considered within the responsibility of the campus security officer.

The haphazard growth that its history signifies forecasts an irregular pattern of authority for the security department of today. The past was one of always being subservient to the voices of the administrator, the faculty, and the off-campus police. To change this mold requires a sharp revision of the laws and policies governing the duties and conduct of the office.

The recent attention devoted to campus security has resulted in the passage of a body of statutory law devoted specifically to campus security officers. These statutes authorize state institutions of higher learning to appoint campus security personnel who will have peace officer[1] authority.

Twenty-seven (27) of the states permit the state governing body for higher education to appoint campus police officers with power to arrest. The remaining 23 states permit deputation of appointment through one of the following: the governor, the court, a law enforcement agency, or by a city government.

Control of traffic and parking is based on the inherent authority of the board of regents or trustees to control the school property and on the statutes specifically authorizing institutional control. Legal arrangements have also been made with contiguous municipalities as to enforcement and judicial disposition.

The extent to which city and county police officers may exercise their authority on campus has not created serious controversy. Jurisdiction over violation of the criminal law has been generally held to be concurrent with that of campus police.

The authority of a campus security officer to search a student dormitory for contraband, without benefit of a search warrant, has changed somewhat in recent years and perhaps greater change is in store. Amidst all the potential conflict areas that exist on a campus, this intrusion ranks high as a source of dissatisfaction.

Search warrants are necessary and must be precise in language, definite in description, and exact in concluding the existence of need.

The college as a "unique" institution and the "in loco parentis" relationship has buttressed the legal attitude in support of the proposition that the student's right to be secure against unreasonable search need not be inviolate. The law views the student as having waived certain rights and as having only temporary use of the dormitory premises.

State Training Programs

Only 2 of the states require or provide special training for campus security on a regular basis. New York with centralized state coordination has established an ongoing training program within the State University System (SUNY), and the 8 campuses of the University of Texas system have their own training academy.

Six (6) states have recently had special short-term training programs available for campus security personnel: The University of Illinois two-week Campus Training Institute, the Iowa Law Enforcement Academy voluntary seminars for private school security officers, the Eastern Kentucky University. one-week Campus Security Workshop, the Maryland Army Reserve Unit's thirty-two hour Crowd Control course, the Tennessee Law Enforcement Training Academy one-week program, and the Utah Division of Peace Office Standards and Training 40 hour in-service Campus Security Course.

Administrative Rules and Policies Concerning The Role of the campus Security Office in Campus Disorder Situations

Many institutions have prescribed rules and policies detailing the course of action required of personnel during disruptive student behavior

The campus security officer role is small or great in these emergency situations depending on factors wholly within the philosophy of the individual college. Contact with the disruptive students is maintained generally be the dean of student affairs. Decision as to the need for outside forces is that of the chief administrator. The campus security officer is sometimes consulted in these situations. He usually performs ministerial tasks such as reading statements of law to students and notifying outside enforcement agencies of the president's request for assistance. In most instances the off-campus police forces assume tactical control of the policing situations, and campus security officers perform under their direction.

Chapter Summary and Conclusions

The legal posture of the campus security office offers the same uncertainty as is suggested in its unsettled historical origins. The legislature has been hesitant to create a full-fledged enforcement officer on campus, and the educational institutions have been wary to delegate the authority they possess. There are few standards established by law for employment among state colleges and virtually none among private colleges. Authority has generally been derived in the past through deputation, and until the law becomes more firm, this practice will probably continue. An examination of colleges and universities detailing the precise duties to be performed in a major campus disorder situation shows the security officer as having a limited and proscribed role. His main function is to serve as liaison between the administration and the off-campus police.

The limited legal support offered by the legislature and the confining policies provided by the educational institution portend a restrained and a restricted campus security operation.

The history and the legal structuring of the campus security position in each of the states have produced a variety of responsibilities. Variables such as the enrollment, the types of institutional control, and the academic level have further influenced the duties assigned to the office. Despite this, there is also much uniformity visible in the organizational structure and in the relationships among components of the educational institution and with outside police forces.

Part-time officers, students and females are used sparingly on campus security staffs and employment benefits generally are limited to a paid vacation and a retirement pension.

Training requirements for security officers are emphasized more at public institutions and at schools in the over 20,000 population bracket. Many of the security officer's duties are of a non-police service function such as responsibility for lost and found, key control, ambulance service, and escort service for visiting dignitaries.

There are few specialists on staff, particularly at the smaller colleges. Outside police agencies are the main sources for intelligence and for the use of undercover agents. Almost all of the security staffs utilize "walkie talkie" communication devices and the student photo I.D. card has general use. Sophisticated detection instruments such as a closed circuit television set and telephone recording devices are rarely found on campus; a large number of schools have no chemical crowd control equipment available.

The campus security officer has minor involvement in policy-making related to student codes of conduct and to student discipline and only infrequently has regular meetings with students. He meets regularly with committees of the administration and with the office of the dean for student affairs. There is a routine exchange of information with the dean for student affairs in regard to students who may be trouble prone. The campus security office participates in student orientation briefings at one half the colleges and is involved in forums and lectures on traffic safety, narcotics and vice, crime, and civil defense at a lesser number of schools.

Students arrested by the local police receive little or no assistance from the campus security office.

The extent to which the campus security office is supportive to students can perhaps be better understood in the context of the relationships existing between the two groups. The ability to communicate, the mutual esteem offered, the kinds of enforcement action imposed upon students, and the manner in which authority is used are all indicators of this relationship.

The role of the campus security officer in disorder situations is conditioned in great part by the behavioral latitudes permitted students, the campus attitudes toward campus security involvement, and the extent of the involvement of the outside enforcement agencies.

The history of the campus security office reflects a variety of service tasks distributed among several functionaries which ultimately came to be housed together. From the early fire-watching days to traffic control and student: disorder, it has been a body generally utilized "for" but rarely considered "of" the university.

The law is well established in regard the right of institutions of higher educations to control traffic and parking within their own disciplinary machinery. The courts have upheld the colleges' imposition of reasonable penalties for such violations and have provided the civil court system as an appeal tribunal.

Adequate legal precedent exists upon which a campus security officer may enter a residence hall in search of contraband without benefit of a search warrant. The case law condoning such entry is predicated upon several theories; the major legal premise is that the institution must be afforded the flexibility of access to all buildings in order to properly govern itself. The student is also considered only a temporary occupant of the premises and by his enrollment "waives" certain rights. The privilege of entry is available to administrators and may be delegated to law enforcement officers in the pursuit of a reasonable investigation. The erosion of the "in loco parentis" doctrine and recent judicial pronouncements suggest that the privilege of entry without a warrant may not be arbitrarily invoked.

The formalized role of the campus security office in major stress situations such as organized or spontaneous campus disorder is to provide intelligence upon which administrators may make decisions, to serve as liaison with outside police agencies, and to gather evidence for later use against students violating the law. Although the press of events may force campus security officers into confrontation situations, the plans for responding to campus disorders do not generally contemplate such a role. The campus security office's early involvement is aimed primarily at delay so that student personnel officers and the executive officer may have the opportunity to use whatever personal, persuasive influence they can marshal. In the event the institutional executive determines that outside force is necessary, the campus security serves as a communications liaison to interpret the tactical decisions demanded by the outside police agencies in terms of the goals aspired to by the executive.

While the complexities of a campus-wide disorder may impose limitations upon the involvement of the security officer, his ability to respond to the normal, foreseeable, routine, enforcement contingencies also remains open to question. The profile of the campus security function discloses many characteristics that suggest only/ a minimal ability to satisfy ordinary campus needs.

All components of the university recognize that the campus security force most effectively performs the tasks requiring the least specialty training. Building and ground patrol, parking, and traffic control are at the top rank, it that order, while the duties involving criminal investigation and student disorders are the areas least effectively performed.

It is apparent to security officers that the presence of larger student bodies, more vehicles on campus, more buildings to patrol, a rise in the individual crime rate, and the potential for disorder arising from student demonstrations call for an increased professional staff.

The working relationship with administrators also extends to outside police agencies. The local police are available for many manpower and investigative services, and in some instances campus violations of the municipal and state law may be handled by security officers within the framework of the school's discipline structure rather than requiring students to face criminal prosecution.

The image of the campus security officer that is transmitted to the student represents order and authority. The uniform, the weapons, and the equipment are synonymous with discipline and control. From the student point of view, the product is not conducive to a mutuality of interest. The absence of joint educational programs and regularly scheduled committee meetings also negates the development of any meaningful interchange. The failure of campus security to offer assistance to students in need of aid as a result of an off-campus arrest may further estrange the two groups. The differential in educational background and age also widens the chasm.

The campus security officer has travelled a considerable distance since the early watchman days, but he need not look too far behind to see that role still beckoning. The crisis on campus has created a void which, with adequate upgrading and new orientation, he may well fill. A revitalization and resurgences can make it not only truly protective of property and person but also supportive of students and contributory to the educational process.

CAMPUS SECURITY

COMMENTARY

This section describes the structure of the campus security office and appraises its function through an examination of its legal apparatus and by the relationships it has maintained with other components of institutional life.

The findings are based upon research in the legal status of the security office and the authority of the security officer; questions as to the structure, the functioning, and the relationships of the security office; and the assessment of the campus security function and its ability to be supportive to students.

In particular, this summary takes cognizance of the inconsequential role heretofore delegated to the security officer and the significant part he may yet play as the threat to the security of the campus accelerates.

1. The history of the campus security office reflects a variety of service tasks distributed among several functionaries which ultimately came to be housed together. From the early fire-watching days to traffic control and student disorder, it has been a body generally utilized "for" but rarely considered "of" the university. Campus security officers and their predecessors have been long cast in roles of menial activities with minimal responsibilities. Never having attained recognition and legitimacy as a part of the total university community, they continue to exercise an uncertain authority amidst a questioning constituency.
2. The uncertainty that has always surrounded the role of the campus security officer is best evidenced in the limitations placed upon his authority. Until recent years few of the state legislatures bestowed direct arrest authority upon a campus security officer. The authority was obtained derivatively as a result of deputization by the local municipal police department or by the sheriff. Although many state legislatures now permit the governing bodies of higher education, such as the boards of regents, to designate campus security officers with peace officers' authority, deputization continues.
3. This situation exists inasmuch as the authority obtained through the governing bodies is usually of a narrow range and it has not yet had the benefit of adequate court testing and judicial approval. Some few states permit private colleges to obtain similar appointments, generally through application to the governor, but the rule among private colleges has been to rely on deputization for their campus security authority.
4. Among the states requiring mandatory training for entering police officers, several do not yet consider a campus security officer subject to the standards imposed upon peace officers. Moreover, the federal government specifically excludes many campus security officers from the benefits of available training scholarships. Virtually no organized, state-wide specialized training programs for campus security officers are either required under the law or are afforded under state auspices.
5. The law is well established in regard the right of institutions of higher educations to control traffic and parking within their own disciplinary machinery. The courts have upheld the colleges' imposition of reasonable penalties for such violations and have provided the civil court system as an appeal tribunal.
6. Adequate legal precedent exists upon which a campus security officer may enter a residence hall in search of contraband without benefit of a search warrant. The

case law condoning such entry is predicated upon several theories. The major legal premise is that the institution must be afforded the flexibility of access to all buildings in order to properly govern itself. The student is also considered only a temporary occupant of the premises and by his enrollment "waives" certain rights. The privilege of entry is available to administrators and may be delegated to law enforcement officers in the pursuit of a reasonable investigation. The erosion of the "in loco parentis" doctrine and recent judicial pronouncements suggest that the privilege of entry without a warrant may not be arbitrarily invoked.

7. The formalized role of the campus security office in major stress situations such as organized or spontaneous campus disorder is to provide intelligence upon which administrators may make decisions, to serve as liaison with outside police agencies, and to gather evidence for later use against students violating the law. Although the press of events may force campus security officers into confrontation situations, the plans for responding to campus disorders do not generally contemplate such a role. The campus security office's early involvement is aimed primarily at delay so that student personnel officers and the executive officer may have the opportunity to use whatever personal, persuasive influence they can marshal. In the event the institutional executive determines that outside force is necessary, the campus security serves as a communications liaison to interpret the tactical decisions demanded by the outside police agencies in terms of the goals aspired to by the executive.

8. While the complexities of a campus-wide disorder may impose limitations upon the involvement of the security officer, his ability to respond to the normal, foreseeable, routine, enforcement contingencies also remains open to question. The profile of the campus security function discloses many characteristics that suggest only a minimal ability to satisfy ordinary campus needs.

9. Particularly among small institutions and especially private colleges, the training is limited, the equipment is meager, and the advantages over the local police nonexistent. The security force generally lacks specialists within the department, has a minimum of sophisticated equipment, and what little intelligence is available is obtained from outside police sources. Students and female officers are scarcely used and only in short demand.

10. All components of the university recognize that the campus security force most effectively performs the tasks requiring the least specialty training. Building and ground patrol, parking, and traffic control are at the top rank, in that order, while the duties involving criminal investigation and student disorders are the areas least effectively performed.

11. It is apparent to security officers that the presence of larger student bodies, more vehicles on campus, more buildings to patrol, a rise in the individual crime rate, and the potential for disorder arising from student demonstrations call for an increased professional staff.

12. Administrative changes are sought by security officers with almost 60.0 percent favoring a centralized, state-wide coordinating body and almost 70.0 percent requesting a chain of command which would lead directly to the president. None of the other respondent groups (faculty, students, administrators) evinces strong support for these propositions.

13. There is no consensus among the campus groups as to the personnel changes which would most improve performance. The security officers and the administrators ranked salary increase as the top priority personnel change, whereas the students and the faculty selected specialized training in human behavior as their first

choice. Inasmuch as the campus security office services a select clientele in a unique setting, the projected changes need not be weighed against the prototype sought for the law enforcement officer employed to exercise order among the general population.

14. The campus security office has virtually no involvement in policy-making beyond traffic regulations and has little contact in a formal setting with students and faculty. A good working relationship seems to exist with the office of student affairs and other administrators as well as with the outside police agencies.

15. The strong support indicated by all four groups (campus security, faculty, students, and administrators) for the proposition that too few channels of communication exist between the campus security office and the students is evidenced by the lack of security officer participation in student educational programs, by the failure of the campus security office to meet regularly with student committees, and by the security office's absence in the process of establishing student codes of conduct and student discipline procedures. Students involved in off-campus arrests cannot look for security office assistance except to a small extent at schools in the under-10,000 population brackets.

16. Although administrative support for the campus security office as a policy-making body is absent, there is evidence showing regular committee meetings with the office of student affairs and other administration groups. A continuing exchange of information exists with the office of student affairs concerning problem students, and a concurring belief is held by all four groups that the administrators and the office of student affairs would support the action of the campus security office in a disorder situation.

17. The working relationship with administrators also extends to outside police agencies. The local police are available for many manpower and investigative services, and, in some instances, campus violations of the municipal and state law may be handled by security officers within the framework of the school's discipline structure rather than requiring students to face criminal prosecution. Despite the amicable ties between the campus security force and the local police, the security officer joined with the other three groups in unequivocally asserting that the over-reaction by outside police agencies was the occurrence most likely to change an orderly student demonstration into a campus disorder.

18. The aspirations of the campus security officer to contribute to the educational goals of the institution and to participate in its traditional customs finds little of a responsive chord among other components on campus. Although 40.0 percent of the security officers considered the aiding of students in the educational process as an appropriate goal, only 18.0 percent of the students and 6.0 percent of the faculty voiced agreement. The campus security officer viewed himself as the interpreter of the function of police agencies in our society, but the concept had only scattered support with the students and the faculty.

19. There was mixed sentiment toward the campus security officer's enforcement role. Some of the characteristics deemed the antithesis of higher education tradition were attributed to him. For instance, all of the groups identified him with an authoritarian enforcement approach. In addition, 50.0 percent of the student were critical of his use of informers and about 25.0 percent of all groups suggested that uniforms be replaced with civilian-like attire. Despite the 70.0 percent of the security officers seeking increased authority, there was a reluctance to increase campus security authority or to allow participation in student discipline policy-making. The suggestion that the campus security office is a policing agency and as such is

unacceptable to the academic community averaged but a 30.0 percent acceptance among all four groups. While the campus security office was not totally repudiated because of its law enforcement posture, nonetheless it has not been afforded peer status by the other components of the campus society.

20. The anticipation that a supportive relationship can be maintained with students while performing enforcement duties is an unfulfilled expectation. This was apparent to all four groups in their over-70.0 percent recognition that duties such as searching residence halls for contraband are inimical to maintaining a compatible association, and, as well, in their almost 50.0 percent recognition of the stress created in using necessary force against student disorders. Duties involving building and grounds patrol, traffic control, and criminal investigation are performed in less strained settings, permitting a more harmonious relationship.

21. The image of the campus security officer that is transmitted to the student represents order and authority. The uniform, the weapons, and the equipment are synonymous with discipline and control. From the student point of view, the product is not conducive to a mutuality of interest. The absence of joint educational programs and regularly scheduled committee meetings also negates the development of any meaningful interchange. The failure of campus security to offer assistance to students in need of aid as a result of an off-campus arrest may further estrange the two groups. The differential in educational background and age also widens the chasm.

22. Students do not go so far as to state that the campus security officer is too low in the status hierarchy to maintain their respect but they strongly favor supervisory controls such as student ombudsmen and a joint faculty-student committee to review the performance of the campus security officer.

23. The campus security officer as presently constituted is not trained to provide supportive services for students, is not given a status role by the administration which would engender a high regard, and does not participate in policy making or become involved in aspects of the educational process.

24. Little recognition is attainable to the security officer other than that arising from his enforcement activities. There are few if any common grounds existing between him and the student from which a symbiotic relationship may develop.

25. In some few critical areas, the results reflected similar percentage support among the four groups. However, the internal consistency check to determine agreement among the four groups within each institution showed that in only 2 of the 16 selected items were there affirmative responses suggesting consistent agreement within each of the schools. The item of greatest support had 82 of the 89 schools with all four groups agreeing to the truism that the campus security goal is to provide protection for property and person.

    Fifty schools had all components in agreement that the overreaction by outside police agencies may change orderly demonstrations into a campus disorder. The other items showed considerably lower internal consistency scores. The diversity of attitude among the component groups that comprise the educational institutions of higher learning and the lack of unanimity within each institution suggest a searching reexamination of the campus security model.

ANSWER SHEET

TEST NO. _____ PART _____ TITLE OF POSITION _____
(AS GIVEN IN EXAMINATION ANNOUNCEMENT - INCLUDE OPTION, IF ANY)

PLACE OF EXAMINATION _____ DATE _____
(CITY OR TOWN)   (STATE)

RATING

USE THE SPECIAL PENCIL.   MAKE GLOSSY BLACK MARKS.

	A	B	C	D	E		A	B	C	D	E		A	B	C	D	E		A	B	C	D	E		A	B	C	D	E
1						26						51						76						101					
2						27						52						77						102					
3						28						53						78						103					
4						29						54						79						104					
5						30						55						80						105					
6						31						56						81						106					
7						32						57						82						107					
8						33						58						83						108					
9						34						59						84						109					
10						35						60						85						110					

Make only ONE mark for each answer.   Additional and stray marks may be counted as mistakes.   In making corrections, erase errors COMPLETELY.

	A	B	C	D	E		A	B	C	D	E		A	B	C	D	E		A	B	C	D	E		A	B	C	D	E
11						36						61						86						111					
12						37						62						87						112					
13						38						63						88						113					
14						39						64						89						114					
15						40						65						90						115					
16						41						66						91						116					
17						42						67						92						117					
18						43						68						93						118					
19						44						69						94						119					
20						45						70						95						120					
21						46						71						96						121					
22						47						72						97						122					
23						48						73						98						123					
24						49						74						99						124					
25						50						75						100						125					

DEC - - 2015

ANSWER SHEET

TEST NO. _____ PART _____ TITLE OF POSITION _____
(AS GIVEN IN EXAMINATION ANNOUNCEMENT - INCLUDE OPTION, IF ANY)

PLACE OF EXAMINATION _____ DATE _____
(CITY OR TOWN)   (STATE)

RATING

USE THE SPECIAL PENCIL.   MAKE GLOSSY BLACK MARKS.

Make only ONE mark for each answer. Additional and stray marks may be counted as mistakes. In making corrections, erase errors COMPLETELY.